LEIF
here's a small
sample of Heritage
Salvage with a bit
of me scattered throughout
maybe we have
things to do together
Cheers
Bug.

HERITAGE SALVAGE

HERITAGE SALVAGE
·RECLAIMED STORIES·

TALES OF REPURPOSING & REPURPOSED TALES BY
Michael "Bug" Deakin

FOREWORD BY
Julia Butterfly Hill

DESIGNED BY
Iain R. Morris

CAMERON
+ COMPANY

Man's reclamation proclamation

SONOMA COUNTY

This Week

gives you a glimpse of what you've been missing in The Press Democrat.

By **KATIE WATTS**
PETALUMA CORRESPONDENT

PETALUMA MAN INTO RECLAMATION

Michael "Bug" Deakin sees a lot of waste in abandoning ~~ings~~. His business, Salvage, finds ways ~~them~~. **p9**

JEFF KAN LEE / The Press Democrat

SAVE IT: Michael "Bug" Deakin has been working on a reality TV show and has produced 10 episodes.

Michael Deakin grew up in a family of 10 kids. "We never threw anything away," he says.

Now 63 and universally called Bug, he has turned that Depression-era mindset into a way of life and a full-time business, Heritage Salvage, where he and his staff reclaim, recycle and reuse old buildings.

In 2000, Deakin was living in Occidental, building custom homes, he says. "One day a client tells me, 'I want this place to look like a hundred-year-old Tuscan villa.' "

Instead of faux painting, he responded, "let's just go out and take down an old barn."

He placed an ad in The Press Democrat. "Wanted: old barns and chicken shacks. Will take down for dollars or clear the site." In two days, he had 36 calls.

Twelve years later, Heritage Salvage sprawls comfortably below McNear Hill at the southern entrance to town. It's an easy, casual place where they practice what Deakin calls "sustainable enthusiasm."

They will handcraft furniture, doors, hat racks, tree houses, even Sopwith Camels, he says with a laugh. They work with individuals and businesses. The Social Club, the new Keller Street restaurant, will feature Heritage Salvage's wood.

Not only is Deakin enthusiastic, he's inventive, idealistic, earnest and patriotic. In addition to Sonoma County barns and chicken coops, he wants to salvage the whole country.

"We need to fix this country the way it got built," he says, "not the way it got broken. It got built by community bartering. Everyone had a task and could share that task with their neighbors.

"According to my work with Professor Google, there are tens of thousands of towns across the country, towns of 3,000 to 5,000 people that have lost their factory, their business, their reason for being."

With no jobs, people leave to seek work and the towns shrink. They leave behind empty houses, falling-down barns, empty warehouses, Deakin says, and the people left behind don't know what to do with them.

"Our task is to attempt to reverse the great disappearing act of the 21st century," he says. "I want to show them they could start a Heritage Salvage."

Deakin sees that new business of salvaging and repurposing old wood as one way to save a dying town, an idea he calls "Reclamation Road."

"It is a movement, a concept, not just a business," he says. "It's also a reality show.

For the past year, Deakin has been filming episodes and has 10 posted on YouTube. He was signed by New York City talent agency N.S. Bienstock and hopes to get "Reclamation Road" on the air.

Says Deakin, "I told them I didn't want to do a schlocky made-up-ending show when this country was in the middle of a crisis. I told them, 'I'll drive you across the country and show you a reality show.' "

In one episode, he describes the dismantling of a barn that has seen better days. In another, he shows the reclaimed school bleachers that are finding new uses as restaurant decor.

Deakin also is looking for small towns in need of help, and he has ideas about how to get them back in working order. The process will be grist for his reality show.

He wants to teach them how to stop the exodus by feeding themselves and their neighbors organically, using Petaluma Bounty as a model.

"I take them a template. This is how they started Tara Firma Farms, for example. It's now a CSA (Community Supported Agriculture) with 900 subscribers.

"I want to bring the template of non-governmental organizations that Petaluma has that work so well here."

He ticks them off. COTS (Committee on the Shelterless), PPSC (Petaluma People Services Center), Daily Acts, Petaluma Bounty, Mentor Me Petaluma are the first that come to mind. And he'll throw in fun community events as well, like the recent Petaluma Music Festival and Rivertown Revival.

"Reclamation Road," he repeats eagerly. "America salvaged, one small town at a time. Hopefully, someone who's reading this will think, 'I know this little town you should come and check out.' "

To nominate a town, see episodes of "Reclamation Road" or get details about Deakin's projects, go to heritagesalvage.com or email reclamationroad@gmail.com.

CONTENTS

DEDICATION

This book is dedicated to my mother, Ivy Thatcher Deakin. Our effervescent storyteller, mother of ten, keeper of the light! When Mom tells a story, everyone listens! This was how I ended up Salvaging Heritage.

When we were growing up in Nelson, British Columbia, Mom had hung this poem on the side of the cupboard on the way into the kitchen. It lived beside the doorjamb where we all got measured each year.

Through fear of taking risks in life
I've missed a lot of fun
The only things that I regret
Are those I have not done

When young Ivy Thatcher left the boarding house where she lived in Vancouver, her landlady asked if she wanted anything as a keepsake. She asked for this quote, cut out of the back page of an old *Readers Digest*, and had it framed.

For forty-some years I've passed this quatrain on to thousands as a Longfellow quote. The irrepressible Katie Watts interviewed me for an article in the *Santa Rosa Press Democrat*, and when I sent her the verse she wrote back: "What a good verse to live by. However, and I hate to burst a lifelong bubble, it isn't Longfellow. He never wrote anything this accessible. Longfellow wrote "Mezzo Cammin," referring to Dante's *Divine Comedy: Inferno*'s opening line, "Nel mezzo del cammin di nostra vita" ("Midway upon the journey of our life"), which says the same thing in a longer, more erudite way.

"My feeling is your mom's four lines were so instantly understandable to anyone they were much harder to forget than dear old HWL, who, frankly, gets pretty maudlin there at the end. (Although ''Twas the 18th of April in '75/Hardly a man is now alive/who remembers that famous day and year' is pretty unforgettable.)"

Thanks, Katie—what a marvelous way to have one's bubble burst. I found out recently it's attributed to one R. McCann. Now I have to find all those thousands of people and correct my quote source!

At the Deakin household we didn't have much money, but we sure had a lot of fun. The only thing that I regret was when brother Patrick and I worked all summer to buy a deep freeze for the house. Ovenjoy bread was selling for twenty loaves for a dollar (!), and Mom stopped baking bread, as store-bought loaves could be frozen. I don't think she regretted it, though.

Salvaged wood was in my blood from an early age. Dad worked for Kootenay Forest Products, and always brought home scraps and odds and ends until we had enough to build a little extra on the house or fashion a picnic-style dinner table out of the planks. He also brought home hitchhikers to share dinner at all times, especially holidays.

If I ever went missing they would go look for me down at Old John's cabin above the orchard, or in the abandoned Victorian farmhouses at the end of the field. I loved crawling around any derelict buildings, always dreaming I would find a treasure. Only later did I realize that the treasure to be found was the building itself!

OPPOSITE TOP, LEFT TO RIGHT: *Grandpa Thatcher struttin';* *Mom Ivy Thatcher Deakin; good ol' Kootenay Forest Products; Nelson BC;* **OPPOSITE BOTTOM:** *Grandma & Grandpa Thatcher in Edmonton boonies with a couple of my future uncles and/or aunts.* **RIGHT:** *My kinda place!*

LEFT TO RIGHT: *My family, circa 1965; Sean, Colleen, Timothy, Valerie, Patrick, Mom, Kathy, Kelly, Dennis, Terry Lou, me.*

CLOCKWISE FROM TOP: *If a butterfly and a goose both fly from San Francisco to Belize, the butterfly usually puts on twice as many miles!* **TOP LEFT:** *The Bus is ready to roll; Miracle Mike and Steve'O, veggie oil mechanix, and a naybor.*

For 738 days ending in December, 1999, Julia Butterfly Hill lived in the canopy of Luna, an ancient redwood tree, to help make the world aware of the plight of old-growth forests. Her courageous act of civil disobedience gained international attention. She continues her fight for environmental and social justice today, and is the author of The Legacy of Luna (2000) and One Makes the Difference: Inspiring Actions that Change our World (2002).

FOREWORD

I met Michael "Bug" Deakin at a festival for ecologically and socially conscious vendors and consumers, where I was a presenter and he was a vendor. He sent me a note to make sure I knew he was there and that he was involved in saving trees and forests by reclaiming and salvaging wood from places like old barns, chicken houses, and wine barrels.

From the moment I met Michael, I loved his effervescent personality and his clear passion for and commitment to his work. I also loved knowing that not only did he salvage wood, but that whenever possible he also salvaged the stories of where the wood came from and how it came to be in his lumberyard.

I recognize that one of our many challenges as a human family is our collective amnesia, combined with our collective attention deficit disorder. We are so disconnected from our past, our present, and our future. And we have no thought, when we make choices, of who, what, and where were impacted at the source of and during the manufacture of a product, and who, what, and where will be impacted when we no longer want or need it.

For many years, I have been asking people, "When you say you are going to 'throw something away' . . . where is *away*?" There is no away. There is only here, now, one Earth we call home, one human family we share.

Michael, through Heritage Salvage, has been working tirelessly to transform people's relationship with "away." There are no throwaway people, no throwaway places, no throwaway species, and no throwaway resources.

Sometime after the festival, I contacted Michael to see if he would be willing to supply donated wood for a touring bus I was transforming into a traveling model of sustainable design. I know that talking about problems and solutions is important, but it sometimes is even more important that we model and create the solutions to the problems and challenges we are facing as a human family. Because much of my work is in touring, sharing the message of caring for the Earth and all the life it supports, I wanted to be able to showcase some of the solutions available to us.

Michael was kind and generous enough to not only say yes to my request, but also to offer that if I could bring the bus to his yard, he would help me work on it. Little did he—or I, for that matter—know what we were getting ourselves into. I will save you all the details, but suffice to say we were thrown one curveball after another.

Early on, I started calling Michael "Bug" and then "Bugaroo," and that name is how I think of him and what I call him to this day. He is Bugaroo and I am Butterfly, and together we are the Insect Intersection. I knew he and I were destined to be friends for life early on, because whenever something would go wrong, Michael would say, "That's no problem. We'll turn it into a feature!"

I love how Bugaroo approaches life and work with the perspective that life is less about what comes our way, and much more about how we choose to view, approach, and respond to what it sends us. Needless to say, we had oh so many opportunities to turn things into "features" on that bus and its wild journey.

Although the bus is no longer in my life (my nonprofit eventually sold it, at a much discounted price, to another nonprofit working to educate and entertain people about sustainability and caring for the Earth and each other), Bugaroo most definitely remains an important part of my life—as are his continued efforts to reclaim the incredible beauty that we so often would otherwise "throw away."

Years ago I wrote a poem, two lines of which are: "So I raise my glass high and toast to the hypocrisy of you / We trade in the old for a cheaper rendition of new." As I look out at our world, filled to overflowing with "cheap," "disposable," and other things we think we "need," I see a world that is in spiritual crisis. We have lost our connection to the Sacred. We have lost our connection to what is truly beautiful in our lives and in our world.

In his own way, Michael Deakin, my one and only Bugaroo, is working to help reconnect people to the beautiful, sacred planet that we live on and with, by reclaiming other people's "trash" and, in so doing, proving what a boundless treasure this Earth and all of its beings are.

Michael and Heritage Salvage are true treasures. I hope you, in turn, treasure this book, and through it see all the "hidden" treasures in your life, our world, and our planet. They are all around us, if we only choose to explore and see with and through the eyes of the sacred, playful, joyous celebration of this life we all share—past, present, and future.

Love, gratitude, and blessings,
Julia Butterfly Hill

ABOVE: *Nature embraces structure; our old home, "6-Mile," Nelson BC;* **BELOW:** *My first ride;* **RIGHT:** *Dad, Paul G. Deakin of the "Champagne Navy."*

PONTIAC **1957** **6 CILINDER**

INTRODUCTION

This book is a whimsical, anecdotal meander through many of the barns and buildings that have been woven into the fabric of my life and what has become Heritage Salvage. Every barn, every building, and every board has a story—if you speak the language. These are the talking stories of these buildings and the places to whence they were repurposed.

I have mentioned some of the people who nurtured me, taught me, inspired me, made me think, and shared a drink! It would take volumes to honor all those that touched me—all the creatures great and small. I feel truly blessed!

From the buildings of my youth through the Vancouver Mudflats, from the Pleasure Faires of the early '70s and the huge timbers for our stage on Grouse Mountain to the grand edifices of the essence of Heritage Salvage, we will show you the meat and potatoes of the restaurants we built, the bars we fashioned, and the tables where we dined.

It is my great honor to regale you with tales of the purpose of these structures. My grand desire is to inspire you to rethink that falling-down old barn into a part of your future; some stories of the things that I am fortunate to wander through every day may give you a glimpse of that.

———◆———

When I began the turn on, tune in, and drop out phase in 1967, my father came down to my basement room and gave me a speech about how "freedom is not the right to do what you want, but the ability to do what you should . . ." (I think I "got" it about ten years later.) He also said I needed to cut my hair and shave my beard—or else! When he came home that evening I had my '57 Pontiac loaded with my gear; he asked what I thought I was doing. "I'm 'or else'-ing," I replied.

Growing up in a small town with a large family and no money had made me want to travel, and off I went. If I were president, I would make everyone take the eleventh grade in a different country so they could see that the rest of the world thinks in myriad different ways, and then come back for grade twelve and pass it on!

After some time living in Vancouver and bouncing around trying to start a business, I gathered three buddies and suggested we get work helping Mo Van Nostrand of Basho Demolition deconstruct and demolish an old tenement building in Vancouver's Chinatown.

At the same time I discovered the possibility of constructing a squatter's shack from recycled wood on a site known as the Mudflats, on a shallow coastal bay off Dollarton Highway in North Vancouver. In this artists' and squatters' community we constructed a four-bedroom, cantilevered loft structure on two large cedar driftwood logs in ten days, built to blend into the surroundings. It was my first house and building project using reclaimed materials. We lived here rent free for some years.

The most famous residents of the Mudflats were Margerie and Malcolm Lowry, from whence he wrote *Under the Volcano*, and Old Mike, the original inhabitant, who had built the coolest woodpile ever. During our tenancy we also resided with whale researcher Dr. Paul Spong; artist Tom Burrows; activist Helen Simpson; Willie Wilson, the first dyed-in-the-wool collector of all things old I ever met; leathersmiths Dan and Wendy Clemens; and us, of course. (I recently spent some time with Dan, who now owns a hotel/café in Puerto Escondido, Mexico: Hotel Casa Dan and the Café Deluxe!)

The Mudflats House was a ten-day lesson in repurposing and stealth building. We had torn down the old, cockroach-infested tenement building in Chinatown and repurposed her so she looked like she had always been there. My collaborators were Stump (Pat Davis), Nazco Phil from the northlands, and Clanky (my old pal Ray Clarke), collectively known as "The Boys." It was a riot.

———◆———

Because of the look and feel of the Mudflats and the notoriety of Willie Wilson, one of the original collectors of everything (especially Victorian accents and house decoration), we were asked to participate in movie sets. Willie was an iconic sort of dreadlocked, pipe-smoking character, who rarely washed much in the way of clothes and never used a hairbrush. The "Deluxe Brothers" (all us artists and builders living at the Mudflats) and the "Out to Lunch Bunch" (the band of yahoos living in Kitsilano) got a job in 1971 working on the movie set of *McCabe and Mrs. Miller*. In the amazing style of Robert Altman, the movie was being shot while the town was being built in the background.

CLOCKWISE FROM TOP:
First mud home built by Stump, Clanky, Nazco Phil & me, Candy on the deck after I had moved on; Old Mike; me commiseratin' w/ Ray "Clanky" Clarke; The Mudflats

WINTER FUEL for
shoreline east of

—George Diack Phot-

king lies on Burrard Inlet   mudflat resident Michael Deakin hefts a load
nd Narrows Bridge.   Lumber is ready to burn after long spell of drying

In the film, Constance Miller (Julie Christie) arrives on an old steam-driven contraption that ends up milling the wood for the dream that is McCabe's, and in wacky Warren Beatty fashion we watch this sleazy gambler trying to grow a town around his trail of bad judgment. The essence of the methodology of Robert Altman left me with an indelible imprint of real-time filmmaking and living and building in the now.

At the same time McCabe was filming, so was *Carnal Knowledge* (with Jack Nicholson, Art Garfunkel, and Candice Bergen), and we got invited to the big wrap party. Willie showed up in his coveralls and handed his gumboots to the valet. The Fireweed Bluegrass Band came with us, set up, and played. We drank and ate and I fell in love with Candice Bergen. After chatting with her for ten minutes I spilled a cocktail on her dress, and quipped as she stormed off, "Well, at least you have something to remember me by!"

Helen Simpson was one of the first dyed-in-the-wool activists I have ever met. Not only did she champion some LSD causes (I think she was the first person to test the Canadian courts over the legality of that substance), but she was one of the first real environmentalists I encountered. Helen was a dynamic force in the Mudflats in the late '60s and early '70s.

UNDER THREAT OF DEMOL

SUN INVESTIGATION FIND

Mud Flats no

FAR LEFT: *Tide's out;* **LEFT:** *Ms. Helen Simpson;* **RIGHT:** *Movin' Day – Willie holds nose while Candy looks good.* **NOTE:** *Activist Len George is the son of Chief Dan.*

WRITS WERE ISSUED against squatters on Maplewood Mudflats by North Vancouver District Council, which seeks to repossess district land on Dollarton Highway. Willie Wilson (centre), named on one of the writs, shows what he thinks of the whole thing, while Ida Burrow (left) holding child, Trinity, Justin and mother Candy Hansen look on with amusement. (Wyng Chow photo)

LEN GEORGE . . . claims land
— George Diack Photo

. . . view of Mud Flats home

YARD HAVEN THREATENED BY CONCRETE

Squatters fear for mud flat wildlife

hanty to

would I go?" she   Paul Spong,

LEFT: *Joni Mitchell on dobro;*
TOP: *Dan Clemens reading Davy Longworth's book;*
ABOVE: *Joni wows the crowd..*

build leafy craft village

OLD BARN THE FOCAL POINT OF MISSION FAIRE . . . it has hand-hewn beams

—Ken Oakes Photo

In the early '70s the Deluxe Brothers presented a Pleasure Faire on an equestrian ranch out in Langley, BC. It was the quintessential Renaissance Faire; how could we go wrong with Joni Mitchell in the crowd? Everything was new, refreshing, nostalgic, a throwback, and effervescent. Paradoxically, in the sense that we all seemed to fit into that heralded era, we felt we were the renaissance of change.

There was a teepee set up for an ancient Native American ritual involving the healing powers of peyote tea. The kettle carried on, with or without us. We were lavished with galloping horses in the full-moon mist and sunrise colors that were heaven-kissed. Joni played and patchouli oil lingered as peace, free love, and good intentions flowered. The Faire turned out to be a great success, and we had built the set and the entry—another exercise by the Deluxe Brothers in film set building with repurposed materials.

———◆———

At about this time I also met Alan Clapp, the idiosyncratic director of BCTV news, who was given an unprecedented half-hour per day there to do as he saw fit. He was a visionary in many ways: from organizing Habitat Forum to his concept of the revitalization of Granville Island, Al always had something going on.

In 1976, Mr. Clapp burst onto the world's stage by organizing the alternative Habitat Forum in abandoned aircraft hangars on Jericho Beach in a venue that also featured "the world's longest bar"—made from recycled wood of course—and which ran in conjunction with the official UN Conference on Human Settlements taking place in Vancouver. The Forum was a smashing success, attended by the likes of Pierre and Margaret Trudeau and their young children, Margaret Mead, and Mother Teresa.

Al was also a boon to my traveling whimsy. When I and a few partners started the English Bay Trading Company in the beautiful bay of the same name in Vancouver, Al would get me on the news, waving my arms about and sporting hats of many countries, talking story and taking people on my quirky adventures in a three-minute news segment.

He was the one who first taught me these tenets: There is nothing like a good news story to advertise your business. And: If you are passionate about it you don't have to act.

We worked together on many things, but always retained an edginess. We got entwined in many projects, but our creative differences and my Aries Ram got in the way of us finishing some—or should I say, my hanging around to finish them.

At Habitat Forum, after meeting Prime Minister Trudeau and diligently carrying out my duties as site foreman, I ended up in a large disagreement over a double-spiral staircase I had designed for the bar. Al refused to bend and I did too, so I got on a plane and flew to Southeast Asia, where I spent the next nine months.

Al, I am glad we had those great, cathartic conversations before you passed. Sometimes the things left unsaid over a quarter century become distilled, yet wonderfully poignant.

He always rode his vision.

RIP Alan Clapp (1930–2012).

LEFT: *Burton Cummings packed 'em in;* OPPOSITE: *So did Buffet and band—and how 'bout those shorts?!*

In 1977 I started North Pacific Presentations with Fred Xavier, the owner of Rohan's Rockpile, where we danced and played out our weekends in Kitsalano, Vancouver. In the summer of '78, along with the Deluxe Bros., we constructed what I consider one of the finest outdoor stages I have ever seen. The "Lighter than Air Fair" took place over a summer on top of Grouse Mountain overlooking Vancouver. The stage was huge. The ladies sewed a bunch of ripstop nylon into two dragons that bit the sun as it settled in the west. The lineup included the likes of Burton Cummings of the Guess Who, Hoyt Axton, Jimmy Buffett and the Coral Reefer Band, Charles Gearheart and the Goose Creek Symphony, Valdy, Shawn Phillips, Bonnie Bramlett, Murray McLaughlan, Jesse Winchester, the Ozark Mountain Daredevils, and—make my heart pound— the beautiful Emmylou Harris.

Martin Mull was the host when Bonnie Bramlett and Shawn Phillips played. Martin's contract rider stipulated that he be provided onstage with an overstuffed chair, a lamp, an end table as tasteless as possible, a dozen beers in green bottles (the only one was Heineken)— and would we please escort all midgets to the front of the stage?

I also remember Hoyt actually stopping a song in the middle of his set: "Hold it, hold it, hold it!" as the band ground to a halt, and Hoyt, steaming, yelled at them all, "Could we play in *key*?"

As the Skyride full of concertgoers wheeled over the top tower, packed and racing, she almost touched the cables from the mighty pendulum effect. Definitely an E-ticket!

Jimmy Buffet took the stage with a cast on his leg. The concert in Paradise Bowl on Grouse Mountain coincided with Buffett's release of "Cheeseburger in Paradise," so the White Spot burger chain jumped in on the promotion. We sold the place out, and had so much fun. I spent a bit of time with Jimmy, and we were constantly getting asked if we were brothers. I like to think that in a sense, we were.

Best Father's Day Ever

For almost forty years I lived with a portion of my heart saved for someone I had never met. I heard from that someone six years ago. I had no inkling I would receive this message via this medium, as Al Gore had not invented the Internet yet! Here is that indescribable email:

Dear Michael,

How do I start this? I suppose if you have ever hoped for this day you will be pleasantly surprised, and if not... I hope you will be somewhat entertained.

My name is Suzy, and on March 27th I will be 38 yrs old; and up until March 23rd 2008 I figured my blue eyes were from the Anderson side and my red hair was a lottery prize from the wee bit o' Scot on my mother's biological tree. But alas, much to my "interested in all things thought-provoking" mind's surprise, my thicket of red hair and my lovely nostril-flaring abilities & attraction to many things Irish are inherent from the fellow that my mom has spoken of often (especially over the past few years). Ah yes, 'tis you.

I write this with a bittersweet heart. Our dad passed on March 16th. He had bravely battled cancer for the past two years. One week later, when my Mom first said the facts out loud to me, I saw the floodgate break on something she had carried for so long. I swear my kaleidoscope brain shuffled at least two dozen thoughts & questions within a period of 30 seconds. My heart cracked, mended, wrenched, and swelled all at the same time.

I am not mad or sad for this chapter in my life. I am overwhelmed at moments with emotion and curiosity.

I feel for my Mom. She is the kindest, strongest, wisest, and most beautiful person I have the privilege to know. And has always said, "Truth is stranger than fiction."

I feel for my Dad. He was a hard man who worked himself ragged for the almost 4 decades to keep his family safe. And I know now he had something in him I could never give him credit for.

I feel for you. I can only imagine where your head & heart are at with this.

For me... this has been the most difficult, strange, incredibly enlightening week of my life thus far. At least it helps to justify my speculations as to my being harvested from a cabbage patch, or the possibility of my two sisters being a 2-for-1 deal at the Farmers Market (hee, hee).

With the amazing, yet intimidating abilities of technology I have been able to take a glimpse into your life. Seems a bit unfair but engrossing none the less. Your creative craftsmanship is truly something to be admired. You are obviously a really neat man with a colorful life, surrounded by great vibes & good people.

So if you choose not to respond to this I will not be offended. I understand that sometimes when time marches on, the drumbeats to which we groove are sometimes out of syncopation.

I am unsure of just how to sign off on this, so I am sending this with Peace, Love & Laughter.

Suzy Anderson

PS. By the way... I love chickens, history, wood, and red barns; I have a garden at the foot of our blue spruce filled with all things old & rusty. And our youngest of 2 sons seems a budding entomologist, with flare-able nostrils and marbled blue eyes. And I think that may be the tip of the iceberg.

CLOCKWISE FROM TOP:
*My first love, Candacé,
mother of Suzy; Suzy;
my "grands" Hayden
and Mason.*

The poem says it all!
Opposite Middle Right: *w/Lynn Wallace on Big Chair;* **Opposite Far Right:** *w/grandkids in Idaho; Candacé and Suzy Q in Glade, BC.*

I had been googled! I cannot tell you all the incredible, seriously choked, heart-rending, unable-to-speak, tear-streaming hallelujahs I felt. I not so calmly replied to her email with a "Holy shit, I'll call you as soon as I get home!"

After waiting forty years, I finally got to meet my daughter, Suzy Q, for the first time.

DNA is an amazing thing. Not only does she write like me and use the same words, she has the same word-mangling tendencies that I do, and does calligraphy in the same style! I was not there to pass on these traits; they got passed on in the DNA. And she does have my nose and my smile.

I cannot take back the nearly forty years that washed under the bridge of time, but I can sure make up for it over the next forty. I mean, she never got to come to work with me, wash my car, or help me build something. We never got to go to a parade, float in a boat, or sing songs together.

The love and beauty that is now our bond is a joy to behold. The nurturing strength of her fabulous mother, who endured many things to build a safe haven for my daughter and her other two daughters, I can only fathom, and I am forever grateful. Thank you so much, Candacé; there are not the words to describe my gratitude.

I picked up my daughter at Lake Pend Oreille in Idaho on the 19th of April, 2008, and we fell in love forevermore. There is nothing like a road trip to get to know someone. She is my one and only child—and did I score! She is a fellow Aries of great strength and creativity.

We spent the first on the Pend Oreille
Then down the great Columbia
We hugged and laughed and cried I say!
Then we stayed a night . . . in Portland, eh?

Sunset on the Oregon Coast
Drove thru the tree past Golden Bear
At River's End we drank a toast:
Petaluma next . . . our sunset post!

The week we filled with much to do
My kid to work, wash the car, and shop
Butter and Egg Parade in the chair with Q
Then a day in a boat . . . on Petaluma Slough.

My radio show and then a date,
Tuesday to the mill and a winery,
"Flowers in Her Hair" across the gate
Day game and the city . . . everywhere late!

Then after ten days of all those firsts
We wandered north and stayed in Bend.
Twelve days has helped to slake our thirst
The floodgates are open . . . the dam has burst!

Suzy Q lives in British Columbia with her mother, Candacé, and my two grandkids, Hayden and Mason.

It is never too early or too late to be a father.

THE SOURCES: SPARKS OF INSPIRATION

Far Left: *My sweet Occidental home;* **Left:** *Morning ritual in Chosica, Peru w/Robert Hyde, 1971;* **Opposite:** *Hiking on an Incan aqueduct in Peru, 1971.*

AMAZON AND OTHER AMAZIN' TREES

I have taken parts of my "retirement" along the way to where I am. I have so far taken seven years off, whenever I had the money, and traveled. I once lived in my house in Occidental for a year, rarely leaving the property. I lived out of my garden, smoked salmon that fisherman brought by, ate whatever goodies friends brought over, and finished off a large wine cellar.

In the early '70s I traveled for five years, sending exotic tapestries and weavings, interesting art, and cool curios back to the English Bay Trading Company, stopping back in Vancouver for a while to make sure I had enough money to keep on journeying. I've always been a traveler, not a tourist. I prefer to find a place I like and settle in, learn the language, meet the people, and grok how they live.

I spent my first two years in South America. I climbed all over Cusco and hung my hat in Machu Picchu (this was before they had guards; we slept in the ruins for two fantastic weeks, exploring and feeling the ancient Incas' blood flow over the rocks). While we were there I kept looking down at the Urubamba River and thinking *that beautiful thread I see way down in the valley is the headwaters of the Amazon, a river three thousand miles long and three hundred miles wide at its mouth, which sends fresh water two hundred and fifty miles out into the ocean.* I had to go.

The rainforest and the Amazon are a continent unto themselves. I found a bruja (female witch doctor), participated in the ethnobotanical rites of Ayahuasca, and got a gig on a paddle-wheeler plying the river. Because I could now speak Spanish, they found I was an asset in talking tourists into coming down the river with us.

The trees of this mighty jungle float by in clumps about the size of football fields. Vines, flowers, monkeys, snakes—the whole gamut of flora and fauna on self-sufficient, temporary islands. To be a boat pilot on the Amazon you must go up and down the river often, as these chunky islands constantly reattach themselves to the riverbank somewhere else down the way, and where there was a zig there's now a zag.

The value of the oxygen-giving essence of this massive jungle cannot be understated. It is the way we presently live on this planet that makes us so unsustainable. As we trash our trees to plant food for an overpopulated planet, our arrogance shows through. It should be the Declaration of *Interdependence* that we celebrate. Life in balance is predicated on the survival of *all* species, and none more so than the great oxygen producer, our main raison d'être (besides H_2O): the tree.

Redwood trees, back in California, are an amazing case in point. They have been around since the Jurassic era, growing by the coast because they catch the fog in the summertime and water themselves. A redwood's needles are curled up at the top like small fists, and they catch the fog and change that fog to life-giving water that drips down the branches to the bottom layers, which are splayed out like an open hand. This creature then proceeds to suck that water through her sap layer to the tune of hundreds of gallons per day. A three-hundred-foot-tall redwood may only have a root system thirteen feet deep, but its capillary-like roots cover vast amounts of ground. If you have ever driven out under the redwoods on a foggy day and seen a dry semicircle on the road surrounded by wet pavement, that is the redwood reaching the water out to her root line. After this fog catcher feeds her root system it then takes twenty-four days for that water to travel up the tree to feed the branch that caught the water in the first place. That is patience!

LEFT: *Plaza de Armas, Lima;* **ABOVE:** *Machu Picchu and S.A. melded my traveling styles for my future whiles;* **BELOW:** *Oona drivin' the '47 Cletrac.*

Ode to Fog Catchers

I wake up to the pitter-patter of rain on the roof.
Outside, the redwood deck is wet and glossy.
The air is misty and damp, as if rain is falling.

But there is no rain,
The clouds are not cleansing the sky to day.
It is the Fog Catchers,
The redwood trees that gather
moisture from the air.

The water seeps into every
pore of the mighty trees,
Moisturizing the bark and
giving nutrients to the tree.
Oh, how I love thee, Fog Catchers.
The way you let drip the extra
moisture to the ground,
And give the air a clean feeling.

The chilliness of the fog and the mist
Gives the home a warm and cozy feeling.
Yet another reason to love blankets and socks.
Oh, how I love thee, Fog Catchers.

Your efficiency
And the way you can get water for yourselves.
No watering cans or hoses are needed.

You are kind and unselfish.
You do not rely solely on water from
the ground through your roots,
Taking the water away from others.
No, you take from the air and the sky,
Giving the rest back to the ground.
Oh, how I love thee, Fog Catchers.

Your beauty and majesty.
Your astounding age and height
overwhelm me with awe.
The sound your needles make
when touched by the wind:
A soft whisper that calms the spirit,
Or a louder talking that makes
one never feel alone.
Oh, how I love thee, Fog Catchers.

—Written by Oona O'Neill
(1992 –) in seventh grade

the amazing similarities between the lifeblood of trees and the juice that we use . . .

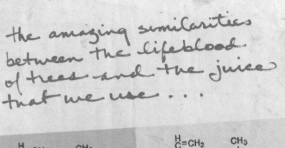

CHLOROPHYLL LIQUID (Plant)

MAGNESIUM

HEMIN—
WHOLE BLOOD (Human)

IRON

© COURTESY OF CATRIONA — "PARTNERING WITH NATURE"

remember . . . we need theirs but they don't need ours. . . . hmmm

mb.

CYCLES OF LIFE

The circulatory system of the tree is similar to that of humans. Even more surprising, the structures of hemoglobin (our life-giving blood) and chlorophyll (the trees' lifeblood, so to speak) are astonishingly similar. The primary difference is that hemoglobin uses iron at the center of the porphyrin ring, while chlorophyll has magnesium at its core.

It is these very trees that have spurred me on to greater practices of sustainability. Whenever I feel unsettled or need a little grounding I always go find my tree. On each property where I have lived, I have a chosen one. I have been doing that for as long as I can remember. The wonderful Catriona MacGregor put it into perspective for me in her book *Partnering with Nature: The Wild Path to Reconnecting with the Earth* (Atria, 2010):

> The Yakuts, Dolgans, and Evenks of Russia, cultures that all practice shamanism, believe that trees are special on Earth because they are the one being that belongs to the three realms: below the earth (roots), upon the earth (trunk), and in the sky (branches). The physical reality of the tree reflects its capacity for binding these corresponding spiritual realms together.

Now, that makes a tree singularly plural in my view!

When you think about it, they are also one of the only species that perform service, supplying our biosphere with life-giving oxygen while scrubbing our constant production of CO_2—very selfless indeed.

Catriona once told a spellbinding story on my *Reclamation Road* radio show, a sometime feature on *The Drive with Steve Jaxon* on KSRO 1350.

Arriving home from work in the early evening and walking into the house, arms full with groceries, her briefcase, and car keys, she noticed that the tree in her front yard was emanating a pulsing light. She trundled her goods into the house and, puzzled, came out to check again, and yes, the tree was glowing. At that time she spent some time with it, but did not in fact interpret it as a message.

The next day when she got home she saw, to her dismay, that the city had removed the tree for whatever reason. There were piles of sawdust and branches strewn about, marking the scene of the crime. The tree had known!

———◆———

I wrote a little volume called *Echo, Eck Ology, Son of Myth Ology*, printed sixty copies, and ran them by a few classrooms of fifth and sixth graders at Salmon Creek School. In it, Echo travels with Muya out in a world congested by cars and fumes and garbage dumps, and as he travels around the country for the first time, having left his place in the woods, he muses:

> I wonder what the trees had done wrong so that they were forced to live by the freeway when their siblings were all dancing on the top of the mountain far away from the noxious CO2 machines. And whatever did they do wrong to be raised on a Christmas tree farm? That tradition actually began as a pagan ritual celebrating Saturnalia, the return of the light, when neighbors would bring a green bough and some candles and share food with their friend. Now it's a dead tree thing.

RE-SOURCE

It's all semantics. In the repurposing business, I consider "resource" to mean reusing our source materials, and then it truly becomes a resource; until then it is an exhaustible source. These magnificent creatures called coast redwoods (*Sequoia sempervirens*) have been in this range in Northern California for the past 20 million years, an incredible show of endurance. There is evidence that close relatives of the redwood thrived in the Jurassic era, 160 million years ago, among the dinosaurs—and who's left? Well, some are here on the Left Coast!!

The old growth redwoods—evergreen, monoecious trees, the tallest living things on Earth, reaching up to 379 feet in height and up to 26 feet in diameter—built most of Northern California. When the first sawmill arrived in California in the 1850s, there were *2 million* acres of old growth. Today there are but 85 thousand.

My, but we are so efficient. We used 96% of the redwood forest in a mere 150 years—after they had thrived for 20 million! Now that we should be coming into our own as conscious co-creators of the universe, it is time we did something about it.

As the brilliant Joseph Campbell might have put it, "We don't need to be looking for meaning in life, but a life that is meaningful."

It would seem that after five billion years of creation we are now capable of contributing to our own evolution, and therefore to the survival and evolution of all living beings. It would be smartest to leave this place in better shape than we found it.

As an artist I felt there were many inspired ways to contribute to this planet—another of our raison d'êtres—and my creativity took me to woodworking. The redwoods dance with my spirit.

Old-growth redwood has amazing properties of resistance to decay. After all, once a tree reaches six hundred–plus years old, it has survived draughts, excessive rain, heat waves, and cold spells, and has become much hardier. Most homes built before 1945 used old-growth lumber in their construction; today most of the trees American logging companies clear-cut for construction lumber range from eight to twenty years old. And these trees can live over two thousand years!

With good maintenance, an old-growth house can last easily 150 years (the oldest wooden structures in Europe are over 700 years old, and in Japan, 1,300). New-growth houses last 20 to 30 if you're lucky. Do the math!

We need to save the remaining forest and add to the old growth—if we all would just leave the hundred-year-old trees in the ground, they would *be* old growth for those who breathe their oxygen a hundred years from now. We know how to do this. Do we have the patience?

The only way to change direction, to do what we must, is step by step. If one does it first, then everyone does it—that is, humanity to the six billionth power.

Chief Dan George

*"The beauty of the trees,
the softness of the air,
the fragrance of the grass,
speaks to me"*

From "My Heart Soars" by Chief Dan George

I was lucky enough in the early 1970s to know Chief Dan George after he had been in *Little Big Man* but before his most endearing role, in *The Outlaw Josey Wales*. He was born in 1899 with the name Geswanouth Slahoot, and in time became the head of the Salish Band of Burrard Inlet, British Columbia. I used to pick him up from the North Shore Hall and drive him home, and we would sit in the dark on the steps of his ramshackle house on the Burrard Reserve and talk story.

Chief Dan oftentimes ended the evening with a quote. It has been attributed to many, but its spirit is quintessentially Native American: "We did not inherit this land from our forefathers; we are borrowing it from our children."

The funniest story among many I heard from and about him was that when he got to the set of *Little Big Man*, Dustin Hoffman was very excited to meet him. "A real chief?" he asked. "Heck, yeah, I want to meet him!" When Chief Dan walked in he was introduced to Hoffman, brusquely shook his hand, and said, "Okay, where's Faye Dunaway?"

Julia Butterfly Hill and Ari Derfel

I first met Julia Butterfly Hill at the Green Festival in San Francisco in 2002. Julia learned the art of public speaking from "Luna," a giant old-growth redwood tree in Humboldt County. To wit, she spent two years on a six-by-six-foot platform 180 feet in the air fighting for that tree's life, protesting against clear-cutting.

She was onstage at the Festival, and there were people lined up to talk to her. I went back to my trade show booth, wrote a note, and stood near the front of the stage while she was speaking. When I garnered her attention I slid the note onto the stage. Julia was so adept at speaking that she did not miss a beat as she bent over and picked up the note, glanced at it, winked at me, and carried on with her speech. I waited at my booth after closing, but she didn't show. I guess she got delayed by her thousands of fans.

The next day I got a telephone call from a very hoarse Butterfly, saying she had stopped at the booth and checked out my literature and would love to get together when she got her voice back.

Shortly thereafter someone donated a vintage Prevost bus to Julia and her Circle of Life Foundation. She wanted to retrofit the diesel engine to run on vegetable oil and remodel the interior as a touring bus. We parked it in between the two chicken barns I was running my business from, and remodeled it in "faux chicken shack." There was a fine flurry of frenzied activity repurposing the "We the Planet" bus.

By the time we finished we had become best friends. Julia stayed at my house, slept on the floor of the chicken barn; after two years 160 feet up a redwood tree, places to sleep in comfort were relative. We talked about a thousand things, and she egged me on to greater Heritage Salvage when she said to some interviewer, "Bug doesn't just stand on the pulpit haranguing people to stop throwing it in the dump, he shows you how beautiful that scrap of wood from a fallen barn can be."

Julia is still making a difference! She has become a bestselling author, and is in high demand as a motivational, environmental, and sustainability teacher. She is still a conscientious tax objector, now living in Belize, though she comes back to the country often for speaking tours. Julia practices another of the *re-s*. She is a re-directionist, and has diverted the taxes she owed to the places she thought they should go: schools, native groups, environmental causes, etc.

Butterfly invited me to a party in the city after the bus was done, and introduced me to Ari Derfel. Ari is the young man who saved all the trash that he generated for one year. He collected all this trash in an apartment in Berkeley, and at the end of that year was celebrated in newspapers and magazines and on network television. It all asked the question, "Where Is 'Away'?"—when you throw something away, where does it go? He was so conscientious in his collecting that when he ordered food to go he would ask them to please not print a receipt because he would have to add it to his ever growing pile of trash. He even filled his backpack in Hawaii and brought it all home with him.

He has since made a large collection of artwork from the trash, and occasionally does speaking engagements surrounding this collection. Ari owns Back to Earth Catering, and founded Gather Restaurant, with partner Eric Fenster and a consortium of friends and investors, in Berkeley. Heritage Salvage built all of the tables and supplied most of the materials. I was very concerned, as they spent a lot of money to open this beautiful restaurant, but it has turned into an unmitigated success. The restaurant was a big part of the Water Tank Waltz. That's just right around the corner, folks, so keep reading.

'BUTTERFLY' HILL LIFE AFTER LUNA

Photos by MARK ARONOFF / The Press Democrat

...k for her eco-bus, Julia "Butterfly" Hill jokes about again working with duct tape, which ...ots of during her two-year stay in the Luna redwood. The bus is being panelled with ...l made from bamboo and also uses recycled redwood from old farm buildings.

the art of re-sourcing
booth 103

garden shed
studio
table
re-sourced wood

100% RECLAIMED BUILDING
HERITAGE SALVAGE.COM
custom design & build 707.874.9010

OPPOSITE CLOCKWISE FROM TOP: *"Fly" and me w/the kids of Valley Vista School; Ari at my BBQ; Ari at HS; me with Butterfly.*

"The question is not 'Can you make a difference?' You already DO make a difference. It's just a matter of what kind of difference you want to make during your life on this planet."
– Julia Butterfly Hill

THE RESOURCES: DANCES WITH WOOD

OLD WOOD MOVES AND GROOVES

HERITAGE SALVAGE

Many moons ago I moved to the wonderful town of Occidental, California—and I loved every minute of it. From Nick Gravenites at Night in Negri's to the Ring of Fire Bike Races down at Taylor Made Farms, the fire department picnics and the yacht club dock parties, to the nicknames of all the quirky characters who live there, Occidental always delights. I learned the joy of not leaving home for days, eating from my garden and daydreaming in the old redwood grove behind my house.

When I first started thinking about Heritage Salvage as my next business venture, I was working on a "Tuscanizing" project in Occidental. We were going to build a fancy Tuscan villa in the vineyards, and I put an ad in the *Press Democrat* newspaper under "Farmers' Forum" saying I was looking for old barns or buildings to take down in exchange for the cleanup. I had over thirty replies. The first barn I got materials from was on an old ranch belonging to the actor Fred MacMurray. I never looked back after that!

Tuscanizing was my style of making a remodel look Tuscan. One of the magical things in Tuscany is that they always built with whatever materials were available. One thing always puzzled me, though: Why were so many of the windows bricked in? The reason turned out to be that the Romans had built many stone edifices with lots of archery windows in them, and homeowners were taxed according to how many windows they had in their house. By then Tuscans were brick makers—hence the look.

After the ad in the paper I began taking down chicken and livestock barns around the county and stashing the goodies at my house. One day my sister Valerie came home and sat on the tailgate of the truck as I was stacking yet another load of barnwood in the yard and said, "Buggy, I'm sure glad you don't have ten acres!"

Lynn Wallace showed me Craig's List for the first time and I found a chicken barn on five acres in Petaluma, and started Heritage Salvage.

In the early stages of the business, running it all from a chicken barn in rural Petaluma, the designer for NapaStyle discovered me, and my relationship with celebrity chef Michael Chiarello began. Besides buying more than two hundred kitchen islands at $800 apiece, he dropped a few gems on my plate. "It's not how much you sell the steak for," he said, "it's what you do with the trimmings!" He is also the one who, after asking me how many hours a week I spent running my business and receiving my answer of fifty-five or sixty, said, "When you walk into a bar, do you talk about your business? When you are in the shower, are you thinking about your business? Well, you probably put in more like seventy hours!"

I moved to Petaluma some time ago, as it was more the size of town I needed in order to grow Heritage Salvage. Though I miss Occidental at times, I do love P-town.

Heritage Salvage isn't just about reusing old wood, but salvaging the heritage of the structures we take down. All of our wood comes with a story. From one of the last wood dairy barns in Point Reyes, for example, we found the salt air from the ocean had actually welded the wood and the nails together (there was no way we were pulling the nails).

We've also taken apart a 600-gallon water tank in Occidental, 5,000- to 30,000-gallon wine tanks here and there, a 50,000-gallon water tank in Yosemite, 100,000-gallon water tanks in Marin, and a 100,000-gallon vinegar tank in Graton. We have "Deakin-structed" buildings ranging from 10×10–foot wood sheds to 120-foot-long chicken shacks, three-story barns in Penngrove, and a grain mill in Crestline, Ohio.

We've got stories, including innumerable tales about Gramps and the million eggs; after the Depression, Granny never threw a thing away—it's all here in the chicken barns, as well as "I remember when you could ride a horse through Sonoma County with your dog and your gun—and nobody cared!"

I was having a ball.

In my continuing effort at "organic pricing," I once had a gent drive up from Danville, California (at the time, the 41st most expensive ZIP code in the country, according to *Forbes*). He arrived in his Humvee looking for some barn wood, barn doors, and various accoutrements to what appeared to be about a $7.5 million remodel. As we found things he wanted I told him I would give him a volume discount, but he kept trying to grind me even more on the prices, until I finally said, "Dude, if you question my pricing one more time I will start adding 10% each time you do." He replied, "Why would you do that?" and I said, "There goes your first 10%. I am running a salvage yard out of a chicken barn and driving a twenty-year-old truck, and

TOP ROW, LEFT TO RIGHT: *Signs by early Bug; Nick Gravenites at 70; instrumental in the Let Bug Stay movement, Ms. Miranda Frederick (left) with her buddy Kathleen Kinmont at my house in Occidental* **ABOVE:** *Occidental supporters at the first Dock Party;* **BELOW, LEFT TO RIGHT:** *My perceptive sister Valerie; The Occidental Yacht Club.*

Letters of Community Support and Charity Acknowledgement for Michael Deakin, aka "Bug"

"The beauty of wood in the state of pleasing decay is one of nature's special masterpieces!"
—Eric Sloane,
An Age of Barns

Top: *Tuscanizing at Thieriots;*
Above: *First HS home (home is where you lay your eggs);*
Left: *Kitchen islands for Napa Style, built in chicken barns for quite a while.*

ABOVE: *Petersen Ranch on Petersen Rd. (c. 1900);* BELOW RIGHT: *Yosemite Water Tank —first of many;* BELOW LEFT: *Sebastopol Fruit Co-op ended up at Hopmonk.*

HERITAGE SALVAGE RECLAIMS 50,000 GALLON REDWOOD WATER TANK FROM YOSEMITE - BUILT IN 1930'S

WoodTalks and Heritage Salvage Listens

World Headquartrs, Petaluma

you arrive in a Humvee, whaddaya think?" He asked, "If I came in my beat-up pickup would you have let me bargain?" I replied, "Well, probably, but you would have to remember to take off your $50,000 Rolex!"

As my business grew and I found myself working seventy-hour weeks, I realized I needed to move closer to my work. This chicken barn was a write-off when I moved into this cool spot, but I transformed it with odds and ends from the yard and now . . . it's World Headquarters!

While we repurposed great old-growth redwood, saving space in landfills as well as a tree or two, I have also learned so much more about the value of this work, and the growing need to use Green building practices in general. It is time for all of us to participate in planet remediation. This is the time of our renaissance and we all need to change 'em up!

Things do evolve through change. The county asked me to move my salvage operation due to a zoning violation. My bucolic agrarian headquarters, consisting of two one-hundred-foot chicken barns on five acres with Petaluma views, became a stepping stone.

The result of an article in the *Argus Courier* prompted someone to suggest that Praetzel's Fine Furniture on Bodega Avenue might be a possible location. These wonderful folks have been there for five generations, selling and repairing furniture since 1951. The lovable Paul and Judy Praetzel were more than willing to work with me. We moved our showroom there and ran it up the zoning flagpole with the county.

I came up with the idea of what I called "Greener E" to establish a "Green" building retail and education center, which would also expand Heritage Salvage's participation in the community and beyond, using the 3 E's: Ecological Energetic Education. We were going to present an ongoing series of hands-on learning experiences: building seminars, organic gardening, off-the-grid power production, and other events to expand the practices of sustainable living. We wanted to learn

from the interns whom we expected to come from programs at the Occidental Arts and Ecology Center, as well as from Sonoma State University.

Greener E was to sell Green building materials and furniture, consult on Green building and design, practice permaculture, and nurture a community organic garden.

Green Fusion Design Center, a San Anselmo, California, firm, was going to join us. Our goal was/ is to decrease our heavy footprint on the planet and to help our communities regain control of their resources. (What I'd really like to do is put a gate in every fence from Petaluma to Bodega Bay so we could all become neighbors again, but don't tell anybody.)

With our lumberyard at a separate location, we were going to outsource our custom work in-county, making agreements with home woodshop owners to build our Green furniture. Meanwhile, we would have our showroom, hardware, garden supplies, and Green furniture at the Greener E. One hundred percent of our wood products are sourced from existing structures that were in danger, abandoned, or no longer being used. Heritage Salvage would resell the lumber, re-mill it, or custom build with it.

Alas, it was not to be. The zoning variances were just too dang difficult and expensive. Then Mr. Mark Gotham of Wind River Partners approached me and offered me a space.

Our mothership has landed in a great place in the best town we could have chosen. A perfect fit! The more time I spend in Petaluma the better I like it. The yard at 1473 Petaluma Blvd. South has grown into my visions of an architectural Disneyland. The space and the crew have melded into a very beautiful, organized, and approachable walkabout. One of the most difficult tasks in the constant inflow and outgo of reclaimed building materials is organizing it, but both the yard and this family I call Heritage Salvage have exceeded my vision.

Wood salvager seeks a home

3-year-old ecofriendly lumber yard must relocate

By TOBIAS YOUNG
THE PRESS DEMOCRAT

In less than three years, Michael Deakin has stacked enough salvaged wood at his hilltop lumber yard to build 18 homes.

That's not counting the wood he's sold, donated for community projects or transformed into rustic furniture.

But now it all has to move.

Deakin's Heritage Salvage company has to find a new home after he ran afoul of county zoning laws that prohibit retail businesses like his in the agricultural-residential setting just west of Petaluma.

Deakin, who goes by the name Bug, gave up a successful custom home-building business a few years ago to start salvaging wood from old chicken coops, homes and warehouses.

His retail shop, fittingly, is operated out of a couple of old chicken coops off Bodega Avenue on Peterson Lane.

The owners of the property liked what Deakin wanted to do, so they've been giving him a good deal on rent.

But now he has to look for new digs.

At first, he panicked at the idea of relocating his stash of wood and establishing his business in a new location. But now he's looking at it as an opportunity to take Heritage Salvage to another level, starting with a more accessible retail space.

"I knew I was probably going to outgrow this eventually," Deakin said.

TURN TO **WOOD**, BACK PAGE

Michael Deakin reclaims building materials and is facing zoning problems at his Petaluma yard.
JEFF KAN LEE / The Press Democrat

WOOD: High prices make search for new place difficult

CONTINUED FROM PAGE P1

To make the move, he's having a big sale this weekend to sell some of his stock.

Deakin said he was given a deadline of about 90 days to find a new place.

That's not an easy task, he said.

Even with a benefactor who is willing to bankroll up to $1 million as a property investment, Deakin said he needs at least one acre — two acres if he partners with a stone seller — with a warehouse or barn for a shop, showroom and some space for indoor lumber storage.

But Petaluma's soaring real estate prices are making property difficult to find or afford, he said.

He wants to stay in Petaluma because he's built up clients and contacts in the community and because some of his best customers come from communities as far away as the South Bay.

"They find it very approachable and accessible, which definitely helps my income," he said.

He's pumped $100,000 of a home equity line into building his business and creating a Web site, and after two years without a profit he's now operating in the black, he said.

What's driving Deakin is a passion for sustainable living and practical environmentalism.

He salvages old lumber from buildings destined for the trash heap to save the tightly grained old-growth redwood and fir in those buildings that can't be found in lumber stores today, he said.

It also means another tree won't have to be cut down, he said.

He advocates recycling and reuse. He drives a 1962 Mercedes that runs on vegetable oil. He has taken time out to help restore old furniture from the Petaluma Heritage Museum for a fund-raiser, build garden beds at the local homeless center, talk about sustainable logging at an Occidental elementary school and transform a public transit bus into a vegetable oil tour bus for environmental activist Julia Butterfly Hill.

Deakin walks around his hilltop location pointing out stacks of lumber and the stories that came with them.

One stack of lumber is from a 50,000-gallon redwood water tank built 75 years ago in Yosemite. Another is wood from a chicken coop in northwest Petaluma, owned by a woman whose friend gave her the property outright in her will, which was a shock to her.

The stories are one reason Deakin loves his work.

"I meet a lot of amazing people every day," he said.

You can reach Staff Writer Tobias Young at 762-9498 or tyoung@pressdemocrat.com.

Going green, saving green

Group honors businesses that find ways to be kind to environment, bottom line at same time

By NATHAN HALVERSON
THE PRESS DEMOCRAT

Michael "Bug" Deakin is a well-connected environmentalist.

In the 1970s, he traveled around with Greenpeace co-founder Bob Hunter, and recently he retrofitted a bus for Julia "Butterfly" Hill, who lived in a tree for two years to stop loggers.

So to some, it might seem peculiar that he was sharing the stage Thursday with representatives from Christopher-son Homes, Infineon Raceway and Agilent Technologies at a business event intended to help companies improve the bottom line.

But with energy, water and material costs on the rise, businesses are increasingly turning to conservation. Increasingly, companies are recognizing that environmentalism and rising profits are not mutually exclusive.

At the sixth annual Business Environmental Alliance breakfast in Rohnert Park, members of the Sonoma County

TURN TO **AWARD**, BACK PAGE

HOW COMPANIES CONSERVE

Some of the ways businesses are saving money while being environmentally friendly:

■ Using compact fluorescent light bulbs, for a savings of about $30 annually per bulb.

■ Installing a solar energy system, which usually pays for itself in about 10 years and provides a safety net from blackouts.

■ Using toilets that consume less water. Dual-flush toilets use from one-third to one-half as much water as regular toilets.

■ Landscaping property with vegetation that requires little or no watering.

AWARDED FOR ENVIRONMENTALISM

... of wood to a customer's truck at Heritage Salvage in Petaluma. Deakin's company, which uses rescued wood for furniture and construction projects, was among 14 companies recognized for incorporating environmentalism into business practices.
SCOTT MANCHESTER / The Press Democrat

STS. PETER AND PAUL
RUSSIAN ORTHODOX CHURCH

Paul Johnson, the Warden, stopped by Heritage Salvage and informed us the church had just bought the property next door to build a cemetery. There were numerous chicken barns and sheds, so my friend Steve Woodward put together a great little crew and masterminded the deconstruction. When I went out to film some of this beautiful chicken barn material with the backdrop of golden onion domes, it was most striking. Paul has a wonderful sense of humor, and as we began talking about the exorbitant cost of burial plots and caskets I mentioned that in Sonoma County they are now legalizing shroud burials. (That is the way I would like to go; let the worms have me.) Then I asked, "At the risk of being blasphemous, as I know the purpose of the typical burial is to be laid to rest for eternity, wouldn't it be a lot less expensive and take up way less room if we buried everyone standing up?" Paul laughed, and said they had had that conversation . . . you never know!

UBUNTU RESTAURANT AND YOGA STUDIO

When the energetic Sandy Lawrence approached me to build some tables and cabinets for a combination yoga studio and vegetarian restaurant in Napa, I was a little taken aback by the combo. What ensued was a delightful marriage of materials and classic food. We first made a community table using slabs from a pair of windfall trees from a 2002 Occidental storm. The redwood trestle legs came from Salmon Creek School and the fir slab tops came from Camp Meeker. Symbiotic windfallery!

As the restaurant and yoga studio grew and I took advantage of some trade—in food, not yoga—I noticed that their cuisine became one of the most photographed I have ever witnessed. A little later, while we were making extra tables and pieces for the annex, Jeremy Fox, their chef extraordinaire, was named one of *Food & Wine* magazine's ten Best New Chefs of 2008, the first in their history to head a vegetarian restaurant.

Jeremy has gone on to other things, but we did make him a box made of food wood to take on *The Martha Stewart Show*. She kept it, dang it! As of this writing the biodynamic Sandy Lawrence has been on sabbatical. I miss those amazing vegetable plates.

TANKS TANGO

REPURPOSING WOODEN TANKS

The fact that wood swells when it holds water out or in has kept us in tanks—and boats! Whether water (redwood tanks), wine (redwood or oak), pickle or vinegar (fir), all tanks are made from clear (i.e., un-knotted) wood. Otherwise the knots would fall out each time the tank dried a little. Each and every stave is clear flat grain, one-quarter sawn, or vertical grain, what have you. Liquids contained within these wooden tanks stain the wood in varying degrees of colors. The longer the tank is used, the deeper the varying stains soak into the stave. Apple cider vinegar gives you a rich brown-to-black patina with a hint of apples and a nose of vinegar for the first couple years. Petite syrah, on the other hand, will lend itself to a fine nose when milled, and gradations of deep red wine soak an inch into the 2⅝" staves. Water leaves streaks of gray and black in the rich tones of the old-growth redwood.

I was asked to look at an old water tank in Yosemite. It was late fall when I went up there, and the snow was falling. The water tank was a viable structure, so I gave them a bid to remove it, and they asked me how long it would take. I replied that it depended on how close to the site my crew could stay. They gave us a three-bedroom house on the Stanislaus River one mile from the tank. I told them we could do it in ten days, and five days later, after the crew and the tank had departed, I had a wonderful stay in the park. Thanks, Bruce!

The 50,000-gallon tank needed to be replaced, as woodpeckers had drilled scads of holes into it. Each hole had been plugged with these beautiful wooden pegs. I concocted a plan to have all the staves fall in, teepee style. It all looked like it would work, until my good pal Steve Woodward missed pulling out one of the plugs. You can still see the last metal band hung up on it at the top. He's made up for that miscue many times over since then.

CLOCKWISE FROM TOP: *Tanks a lot—in Penngrove she held water; in Graton Manzana made their vinegar; in foudres of oak sat wine to soak; picklewood skins; Chris Cheek sketch of woodpeckers and pegs; Yosemite tank in various stages; Steve Woodward leaves one on ladders w/legs.*

Good Food...

Good Friends...

Good Times...

RISIBISI

Risibisi in Petaluma was the first restaurant we did. The co-owners, Marco Palmieri and chef Fabio Flagiello, sauntered into the yard, looking for something interesting with which to remodel the space they had just leased. It was during the World Cup of 2006, and while we worked on it the Italians won! At times it was, shall we say, difficult to get the owner's attention.

We went and checked out the space. Marco uncovered a wall; they asked me about flooring, and we took a sander to the black paint and voila—a beautiful cherrywood floor lay shimmering underneath! Next was the bar and back bar. I had skinned the Yosemite water tank staves for some clear paneling for another client, and Marco and Fabio immediately went for the look. When you stagger the band marks in the staves it gives the appearance of giant weathered bamboo.

We repurposed an old barn door for a partition to the party room in the back, and since then we keep adding various things: a giant mirror, some creative metal accents, a front window sculpture, a stealth awning, a water tank band candelabra. In the bathroom you will find the newspaper headlines of the results of the World Cup.

We recently held the world premiere of the *Empty Denim* video, the anthem for *Reclamation Road*, in this very restaurant.

WATER TANK WALTZ

The County of Marin put the 100,000-gallon tank from Dominican College out for removal bid; I submitted a bid of $1,700, figuring I would get it as the lowest bidder. I did not hear back, so I called the engineer and offered to take it down for $1. The rest, as they say, is history. There were 8,000 board feet of clear staves and a tank bottom 2¾" thick.

We brought the mobile mill in with Merle Reuser, the daffodil man. Merle has since retired from milling and wants to make Sonoma County the daffodil capital of the world by giving away daffodils. We milled ½" skins with all the tank band's marks on them and put them aside, then took the staves to NuForest and milled some beautiful shiplap paneling. They used the paneling on the exterior of Fire Station #2, a very fancy Green-built firehouse in Windsor.

Marin

Recycled redwood put to creative uses

alvaged material from old water tank rned into tables, paneling, mantels

im Welte
n Independent Journal

75-year-old, 100,000-
on Marin Municipal
ter District wooden
er tank that was taken
n in San Rafael last year
s on in restaurant tables,
skey bar walls, fire house
ries and trellises, tables,
lves, paneling, shelving
mantels throughout
rin and the Bay Area.

Michael "Bug" Deakin,
nder of the Heritage Sal-
e building-materials-re-
ling yard in Petaluma,
de it happen.

When the water district
the tank's deconstruc-
n out to bid in summer
8, all of the bids submit-
were too pricey for the
trict's coffers. So the
ial junkman lowered his
to $1.

I'm into salvaging the
ritage wood," Deakin
d. "I'm into the story of
ere it came from and what
ppened to it, so this tank
de perfect sense for us."

Deakin worked with a
ntractor to demolish the
pty 20-foot-high tank,
ich once held 1 mil-
n pounds of water. He
ught the wood to his
taluma salvage yard,
ich has about 350,000 to
0,000 board feet of wood
claimed from demolished
ructures like the water
nk, as well as homes and
nd-felled trees. Over the
xt 16 months, Deakin
oceeded to disperse it to

IJ photos/Jeff Vendsel

John Priest shows off the redwood mantel over the fireplace in his Mill Valley residence. The wood came from a water tank (at top) that was taken down a year ago. The wood went to a Petaluma salvage yard, where it was sold for a variety of projects.

nearly two dozen construction projects.

District spokeswoman
Libby Pischel said that
finding a reuse for the wood
from the district's old tanks
is always a priority.

"Whenever we remove
a redwood tank, we make
sure that the wood is repurposed," she said.

The wood was turned into
a 26-foot curved bar at Mar-

tins West Gastropub in Redwood City, entry panels for
Fire Station No. 2 in Windsor, and the bulk of the interior of Rickhouse, a speak-
easy-style bar on Kearny
Street in San Francisco.

It was also incorporated
into a number of residen-
tial projects. John Priest of
Mill Valley used some of the
wood to construct a mantle
above his fireplace and said

he loved the redwood's "finished look in the end, its
age, its stains, and the history behind it. It seemed ap-
propriate in Marin to have a
redwood mantle."

The home for the final
batch of wood was Gather,
a new Berkeley restaurant
that used the old-growth
redwood as table tops, counter front and entry-door
panels.

Deakin recently celebrat-
ed the occasion by taking
his nine employees on a bus
tour of many of the places
where the wood ended up,
including Rickhouse, Mar-
tins West and Gather.

"But not the fire house in
Windsor," he said. "They
don't serve drinks there."

Contact Jim Welte via e-mail at
jwelte@marinij.com

RICKHOUSE IN SAN FRANCISCO

Daithí Donnelly and Brian Sheehy, the irrepressible Irish leaders of the Future Bar Revolution, came looking for wood (and a story) to panel the interior walls for Rickhouse. I suggested the water tank skins from the hills above Dominican College. Daithí insisted on a story involving whiskey, so . . . the story was that the nuns had a distillery inside the 100,000-gallon tank (that's 20' high and 32' in diameter) and sold the whiskey out the back door to fund the college during Prohibition! Daithí (pron. DA-hee; a Gaelic form of David) has since taken his evening Guinness to the clouds! The bartenders all tell the story to this day.

"I sort of kept my hand in writing and went to work for the Sierra Club in '52, walked the plank there in '69, and founded Friends of the Earth and the League of Conservation Voters after that." – David R. Brower

GATHER

When the ever humorous Ari Derfel came out to the yard to talk about their new restaurant in the David Brower Center, I was really pleased to consider it. It was a new, very Green building named after the great environmentalist, who is credited with inventing the coffee table book as a tool to fundraise for the Sierra Club.

David also had started the Earth Island Institute, and it seemed very fitting that Ari should build a restaurant in such a place. So Ari and partner Eric

Fenster said they would fundraise over a million bucks to build a really cool restaurant, and I'm going, "Over a million—are you guys sure? This is right across the street from Cal Berkeley!"

Well, they spent a lot of money at our place, and they spent a lot of time committing their staff and their plan to sustainability. They cared about the origins of everything, and it shows. And it worked. The place has been rockin' ever since. And it is beautiful! From the front doors out of water tank wood to tabletops of water tank, bleacher board, and windfall fir. Live-edge fir bar tops. Always the question: how far away did this come from? Is it local? Did I mention it was beautiful?

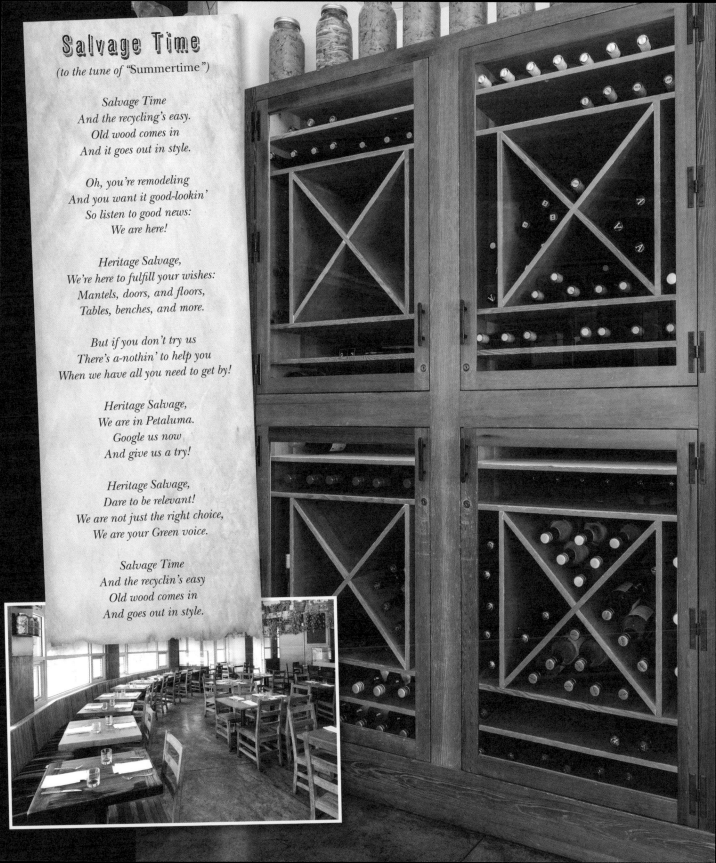

Salvage Time
(to the tune of "Summertime")

Salvage Time
And the recycling's easy.
Old wood comes in
And it goes out in style.

Oh, you're remodeling
And you want it good-lookin'
So listen to good news:
We are here!

Heritage Salvage,
We're here to fulfill your wishes:
Mantels, doors, and floors,
Tables, benches, and more.

But if you don't try us
There's a-nothin' to help you
When we have all you need to get by!

Heritage Salvage,
We are in Petaluma.
Google us now
And give us a try!

Heritage Salvage,
Dare to be relevant!
We are not just the right choice,
We are your Green voice.

Salvage Time
And the recyclin's easy
Old wood comes in
And goes out in style.

"*I love collaboration! Working with Bug at Heritage Salvage was so much fun. His enthusiasm is contagious, and I appreciate that he could see what I wanted and take it to the next level. Love the finished product, and we get great compliments on our new patio daily. I will be lucky if I get the opportunity to do another project with him at some point down the road. He is one of those rare people that I meet who has a strong connection with his right and his left brain; the creativity is magical and the execution is ingenious!*"
—Sondra Bernstein, proprietor, the girl & the fig

THE GIRL AND THE FIG

Sondra Bernstein, the owner of "the girl and the fig" in Sonoma, came by to talk about reworking the patio. She asked if I would collaborate on design. Well, shucks, I love doing that, and with such a renowned restaurateur, author, speaker, and traveler as Sondra, 'twould be an honor! "You and I can do it, can't we?" she asked. We came up with a plan to perform an extreme makeover of the patio: a custom fence with sliding corrugated metal panels, an outdoor bussing stand, banquettes, and a custom entry door.

My sources were the Spring Lake Park changing rooms' redwood and the Penngrove water tank wood—and rusty corrugated roof metal from a chicken barn.

When we started installing the complex series of sliding panels and rusty corrugated metal, the neighbors were concerned about the "Tijuana look," but after we finished, they were pleased. We went a little overboard on the patio entrance door.

MARTINS WEST

Moira Beveridge and Michael Dotson approached me with their plans for a "gastropub" in Redwood City; I got very excited by their enthusiasm and their willingness to design the space around what we had available. The space had six large columns down the center, brick walls, and had been a saloon-slash-theater for many moons.

The Alhambra Theater had been built in 1895 and miraculously survived the Great San Francisco Earthquake and Fire of 1906. It was billed as the finest theater south of San Francisco. It also included a bar and a restaurant that entertained fine ladies and gentlemen.

One such "gentleman" and frequent patron was none other than the famous lawman/outlaw Wyatt Earp. His wife, Josie Earp, sang there, and he would come to see her perform and have some whiskey later at the saloon. In fact, they had a large photo of Wyatt Earp standing at the bar when it was the Alhambra Theater.

I found time to visit the historic building, and we began formulating a plan. Moira and Michael came by a couple of Saturday afternoons at closing, and we would sip wine and walk about the yard, contemplating the meld of materials I had that related to ingredients in a restaurant, including the Dominican water tank for the bar and bar front.

We used the huge metal rings from the water tank for the foot rails at the bar, around the pillars, as tank wrap for the bar front, and to hang the curtains. The flooring was Moscow, Idaho, shiplap. We made the tables from walnut slabs, oak wine barrels big and small, and French white oak flavor sticks for wainscoting. The doors came from these ancient vertical-grain fir door blanks we had found stored in a dairy barn, and the restroom stall doors were from prune trays.

This was and still is one of our biggest contracts. After our summer and fall meetings we kept busy most of the winter making all the ingredients for Martins West. We finally went down there with four carpenters, two welders, and three trucks, and threw most of it together ourselves.

BELOW: *Michael Dotson and Moira Beveridge Dotson.*

TANK NO 20
STOR CAP:
29.791 GALS
112729 HLS

DANGER
CONFINED SPACE
DO NOT
ENTER

LIFE IS TOO
SHORT TO DRINK
CHEAP WINE

FOPPIANO VINEYARDS

Founded in 1896 by Giovanni Foppiano, this is one of Sonoma County's oldest continually operated, family-owned wineries. The family has supplied Northern California with wine for over a century, surviving Prohibition in the 1920s by selling home winemaking kits. Louis J. Foppiano recently left his wine glass at the vineyard and moved on, after living more than a century.

We have enjoyed a long relationship with the large, beautiful redwood wine tanks we got from this maker of heralded Petite Syrah. The old-growth clear redwood from these burgeoning barrels of long-fermented grapes has been used for an eclectic array of furnishings, installations, and art. I've been dealing with the ever helpful and gracious Paul Foppiano, vineyards manager and man of many hats.

We have repurposed copious numbers of tanks over the years. From an iconic surfboard shaper in Lahaina, Maui, to wedding arches, restaurant tables, bar tops, and art pieces, this wine tank wood doth travel!

Right: *Louis J. Foppiano.*

TANK NO 1
STO____AP:
4,0__ GALS
154.31 HLS

DANGER
CONFINED SPACE
DO NOT
ENTER

LEFT: *Ole classic w/Foppiano redwood;* **RIGHT, FROM TOP:** *My goddaughter, Kelly Robinson, talking story; Ole still shaping!*

SURF'S UP!

"Dr. Mike" was wandering about the yard, and seemed focused on the red-wine tank wood, ruminating on its potential use as surfboards. He was going to send them to Maui. It sounded cool, but I never really thought about it—until he came back for a much bigger pile. "So who is making the boards?" I asked. "Oh," he exclaimed, "Ole himself!" Well, after I got educated I had to go and see what this was all about. Bob "Ole" Olsen, a legendary surfboard shaper, still doin' it at seventy-nine years young!

In April of 2013 I put a package together and sent it to Ole. He intimated that it was to be his last one, so I sent him some extra because I was hoping he might make me one. Ole is so much fun to hang with. He used to teach woodshop—and is missing a couple of digits, of course. When this iconic surfboard shaper/surfer enters the water in Lahaina, all the surfers stand off their boards and wait for him to catch his wave: the ultimate in respect. Ole has built boards for Jimmy Buffet, Maui Jim, Duke's, and collectors everywhere.

HOPS AND HOMINY

When a trio of young men from Florida wandered into Heritage Salvage and said they were going to open a Southern food–hipster sort of restaurant in an alley off Union Square, I was thinking, hmm, they look too young to know much about restaurateuring. Well, we had a lot of fun designing around the cool materials we had. They focused on the Foppiano tank wood for the bar and tables, and we did an inlay of hop wood from the Hops Warehouse on each table—and they are kickin' it down that alley! Congrats to Daniel, David, and Adam!

SHIPLAP SHUFFLE

From Floor to Ceiling with Old Mill Wood

The first commercial venue we laid shiplap flooring in was the Martins West Gastro Pub in Redwood City (p. 62). Shiplap is wooden sheathing in which the boards are rabbeted so that the edges of each board lap over the edges of adjacent boards to make the joint flush. It is so called because it was a boon to shipbuilders, as it took much less caulking to keep the swelled joints of a boat seaworthy.

The first time our friend Len showed up in the yard with a load of shiplap from a granary in Moscow, Idaho, we noodled on how to market this plentiful product. We decided it could be flooring, but we would need to re-educate the public and the flooring contractors as to how it would work. Because of the nature of shiplap, it would have to be face-nailed on one side—but it already had nail holes in it.

The first load of shiplap I sold as flooring was to a young lady in Occidental. She then called Scott Hickey, a flooring contractor, to lay the floor for her. After he looked at the material he called and indignantly asked, "You call this flooring?"

In the years since, he has become a huge fan of reclaimed flooring and shiplap in particular. In fact, he renamed his company Heritage Flooring.

We cannot keep up with the demand for shiplap flooring, so now our supplier in Washington mills it all from huge wooden grain elevators, built circa 1936 and measuring 36'×48'×80' with flat, stacked walls made of 2"-thick material and a capacity of 77,000 bushels of grain; we mill two boards from each plank. There were approximately 175,000 BF of lumber used in the construction, with about 130,000 BF salvageable. Wooden elevators were flat-stacked to contain the huge tonnage and downward pressure of all that grain.

Harper enjoys playing on the shiplap floor laid by parents Arann Harris and Paige Green.

SHIPLAP

A

B

5/16
3/8
5/16

5/16
3/8
5/16

NOMINAL SIZE	A	B
1 X 5	4⅞	4½
1 X 7	6¾	6⅜

ABOVE: *Profile of shiplap as most versatile product;* **THIS PAGE:** *Floors by Scott Hickey w/Rex the floor dog;* **OPPOSITE:** *Audrey and Wesley enjoy their shiplap floor.*

HERITAGE SALVAGE .com

BUILDING MATERIALS

Reclaimed Flooring
DOGGONE BEAUTIFUL!

Rex makes his stand on sustainability!
823-9999

www.heritagesalvage.com
1473 Petaluma Blvd S, Petaluma 94952 -(707) 762-6277

Tom Waits

The first day Tom Waits came to the yard I wandered about with him and Peter, his contractor, swappin' talkin' stories and testing various woods for sound quality: redwood sticks, tamarack, fir, and walnut among other things. As we grew to know each other a little, he would bring his notebook with him, and he wrote down a few of the anecdotes that are in this book. He bought some shiplap and some flooring that made it into his cool studio in West Sonoma County. He used to love coming by to peruse the stock of doors, telling me he did doors in a different order than most: He preferred buying doors and finding doorways for them later!

I was lucky enough to hear some of his great stories, and I am forever awed by his talent to put a topical moment into a song that resonates with indignation and soul. I got to take my daughter for a tour of his studio, and his collection of pianos and sundry music-makers is as idiosyncratic as the minstrel man himself. Tom put some of the Moscow, Idaho, granary into his music studios. The doors are still waiting for doorways.

ABOVE: *Peter Swanhuyser, builder extraordinaire, w/Tom Waits at HS;* **LEFT:** *The Vault—Treasures of the Quirky Bard.* **BELOW:** *my Suzy Q at Tom's studio;*

HOPS SCOTCH
From a Washington Hops Warehouse to Breweries and More

From this Irishman's point of view, one of the very honorable functions of a building is coddling the ingredients of one of my favorite libations. One of the Lords of the Hop was John I. Haas, who set up his hop operation in Yakima, Washington. His Golding Hops Warehouse, located in Buena (Zillah), Washington, just down the road from Yakima, was built circa 1920. The building was constructed in four sections, with large cooler doors and insulated brick walls dividing each section. Outer and cross walls were of brick, with wood shavings for insulation on the inside of the wall, held in place with shiplap, framed twelve inches from the brick. The attic was insulated similarly, with thirty-six inches of shavings. The building was two stories high, 325 feet long and 75 feet wide.

Cooling and air circulation were provided by two systems: a 6-head 50-horse ammonia compressor for cooling, connected with two large fan cages powered with 10-hp motors ducted throughout the building to move the cooled air. Each section was designed to hold up to two hundred tons of hops. Each floor was also insulated with twelve inches of shavings, held in place with shiplap on the ceiling below.

There was a box belt to move the boxed hops from packing on the second floor to waiting trucks or railcars outside a sliding door on the first floor. Originally, the rollers for the belt were of wood. At the time of deconstruction, there were still a few wooden rollers in place, and the box belt was active and worked fine.

The lineup of destinations for this repurposed warehouse of hops is stellar! Lagunitas Brewing Company in Petaluma, three Hopmonk taverns, seven restaurants, wineries, and many homes!

LAGUNITAS BREWERY
Hops and Props!

I first got to know the Lagunitas gang because I was putting on a dock party with the Occidental Yacht Club, "where you need not own a yacht to be a member, you just got to be a little dinghy!" I had started the yacht club with Bruce Bordi and Bob Black, and it was designed to be a social and service organization that gave all profits back to Occidental charities. I asked Ron Lindenbusch (Chief Marketing Officer) for a donation of beer. He said, oh, we know how Occidental parties, you better take at least six kegs, and just in case, here's my phone number for when you run out. Well, we ran out; he said to run across the street and get a couple from Gerard at the Bohemian Café, and tell him we'd replace them tomorrow. That, my friends, is service and dedication to donating beer as a sustainable marketing plan!

The shiplap from the Yakima Hops warehouse was used throughout as wainscoting. The altar from the Church of the Salvaged Log (a windfall redwood tree) became a beautiful checkout stand in their store, and their bar comes from the bar in the officer's club in the George Lucas movie *Red Tails*. There are other pieces from the movie, including benches and a table from the mess hall, the POW camp, and chairs, all of which were first assembled and filmed in the Czech Republic.

Tony Magee, the founder, actually lived in Lagunitas when he brewed his first beer on his kitchen stove. Then Carissa, his wife, kicked his brewing operation out. I think that was when he started in earnest in Forest Knolls before he outgrew the septic system and came looking for Petaluma.

The dog on the label? Tony told me on my radio show that although everyone wants to see the dog stuffed on a shelf in the beer lounge with some cool family dog story, he actually cut it out of the back of a magazine and stuck it on.

HOPS AND PROPS!

FROM FAMED HOPS WAREHOUSE IN YAKIMA, WA
TO LAGUNITAS BREWERY, HISTORIC PIECES HOLD THEIR OWN.

YAKIMA GOLDING FARMS WAREHOUSE
JOHN I. HAAS INC.

The Golding Hops Warehouse located at Buena (Zillah), Wa. It was built circa 1920. The building was constructed in 4 sections; with large cooler doors and insulated brick walls dividing each section. Outer and cross walls were of brick with wood shavings for insulation on the inside of the wall.

The shavings were held in place with shiplap, framed 12 inches from the brick. This shiplap is throughout Lagunitas, wainscoting in the Stores, the Tap Room and paneling in the lounge. The attic was insulated similarly, with 36 inches of shavings. The building was 325' long by 75 feet wide, two stories high.

Each section was designed to hold up to 200 tons. Each floor was also insulated with 12 inches of shavings, held in place with shiplap on the ceiling below. Again this shiplap has appeared all over Lagunitas including here in the store, at Hopmonk Sonoma, restaurants and wineries!

Cooling and air circulation were provided by two systems: a 6-head 50 horse ammonia compressor for cooling, connected with two large fan cages powered with 10 horse motors ducted throughout the building to move the cooled air.

This is the original church of the Salvaged Log, the church is still there but Tony Lagunitas made me an offer for the altar I didn't understand, and I took it!

The Altar from the Church of the Salvaged Log was rescued from this windfall tree. Felled by the storms of 2002 in Occidental

There are other pieces from the movie set, including the benches and tables from the Mess hall, POW camp and chairs from the Airmen's Camp in Italy. These were first assembled and filmed in Czechoslovakia!

The Bar in the Store was the Bar from the Officers Club in the George Lucas movie, Red Tails, the story of the Tuskegee Airmen!

LAGUNITAS BREWING COMPANY PETALUMA CALIF.

WALDO MEMORIAL HALL

LAGUNITAS BREWING · PETALUMA CALIF.

PREVIOUS PAGE: *w/Dr. Cerveza (Ron Lindenbusch);* **RIGHT:** *Shiplap and beer;* **ABOVE:** *Ales and Tales, swag in the bag, but Where's Waldo?*

FARMHOUSE ALE

LAGUNITAS BREWING COMPANY · PETALUMA CALIF.

WILD GOAT BISTRO

Nancy Delorenzo came through the yard a few times before we warmed to each other. My prices didn't fit her budget, so we worked at finding a middle ground. After a few visits, design consultation, and some price haggling, we arrived at mutual respect, which has turned in to a full-on "We love Nancy and her Wild Goats." Her café became an instant success, and Petaluma loves every bit of it. We put in the floor and then made a sign and a really fun menu lectern and the benches for the breezeway table and then and then . . . one of our favorite parts of the Wild Goat Bistro is when we get to do something else and take Friday lunch pizza in trade.

BUILD PIZZERIA ROMA

Dean Biersch recommended to restaurateur Lisa Holt that she come see us to supply flooring and tables for Build, which was inspired by Italian pizzerias with their sense of community. It is located at 2286 Shattuck Avenue in Berkeley in a landmark 1904 building. "Find Your Inner Pizza" in this fabulous space where Lisa and partner/husband David Shapiro really made a splash with how they "built" Build with Heritage Salvage wood. Who woulda thunk that used building materials could be so elegant in a pizza joint? Between the shiplap flooring, Pony Express wood for the tables, and metalwork styled by our own Dave Rawson, they totally nailed it. Figuratively as well as literally.

GALETTE 88

There is nothing that speaks to me like a savory crêpe! When Celine Guillou and Erin Rooney first approached me about flooring for their space I was tickled that it was in the same building as Rickhouse. Also, it seems very French (as the wonderful Celine is) to walk down a wee alley and find a fabulous crêpe. After having worked on various things for Celine over the years, we had fun figuring out their plan. We were going to wrap the beams, but after smacking a hole in the original wrap we found some beautiful, riveted, honkin' I-beams. So we sashayed in with hops flooring and Camp Meeker windfall slabs instead.

BOCA PIZZERIA

By the time Boca Novato came along we were nearing the end of the Hops Warehouse shiplap, and their contractor Joseph up and bought everything we had left. We made very creative usage on the ceilings by gapping the shiplap about four inches apart throughout, thereby stretching the amount.

We had no original shiplap left, but had begun milling our own from grain elevators in the Pacific Northwest. That did not slow them down for a minute. They were not shy about shiplap, as you will see here in Boca Corte Madera . . . everything from the bar tops to the booths, the hostess stand to the walls, and the now-trademark ceiling.

PUB REPUBLIC

Jory and Mark Bergman came into Heritage Salvage one day and said they were taking over the Albatross at 3120 Lakeville Hwy in Petaluma. This location had seen many failed attempts at restaurants, its last iteration being Zocolos. We remodeled it with a complete suite of shiplap wall treatments, sliding barn-style doors, community tables, and a bleacher-board entrance feature. With a forty-something-foot bar and back-bar accents we warmed the interior of the place up. Jory and Mark then added craft beers, excellent food, and some great wines, and they have not looked back since.

The Prune Tray Shuffle

So a wonderful female client arrives with her designer, doing a remodel on her vacation home in beautiful West Sonoma. We spend a couple hours going over the plans and choosing materials; both she and her designer turning out to be delightfully creative people. Amongst the many things she chooses are about thirty prune trays, for which I charge her $30 apiece.

While they are looking at some other things, a young accordion player shows up in his twenty-five-year-old station wagon, looking for seven prune trays to build a privacy screen around the porch of his first house, which he and his young family have purchased in Rio Nido (very inexpensive real estate), and I charge him $15 each.

The woman hears me and says, "Wait a minute, Bug, I'm buying thirty and he's buying seven, and he pays half of what I am?!"

I say, "Come out here, guys," and point to their Lexus SUV and Mercedes, and then point at his car and say, "Whaddya think? Your two vehicles are probably worth what his house is!"

She very graciously says, "That makes all the sense in the world, Bug, carry on."

Prune Trays and Wine

Although our shop was just a little chicken barn in West Petaluma, I was approached by the exclusive Harlan Estate for some room divider/shoji screen–type pieces that we had invented using prune trays. Two days before we were to deliver the screens, the Estate called up and asked if we could make three extra. I whined that this was very short notice, and Harlan's executive assistant Lisa Savano said, "Charge whatever you want!" So I charged them double for the rush job, and said I wanted some wine also. About a month later Lisa brought me two bottles of wine and dropped them on my desk. "All I get is two bottles for performing at such short notice?!" I wailed. "Well, Bug," she replied, "They are worth $600 each!"

"Can I get twelve $100 bottles instead?" I joked. (But I must admit they were spectacular.)

SOUTHPAW BBQ

When that Southern belle Ms. Elizabeth Wells first sashayed into the yard looking for material for her proposed Southern BBQ restaurant in the Mission district in San Francisco, we knew we were going to get to play outside the proverbial box. I would call our collaborative end result "simple elegance." We had some hacked but beautiful Claro Walnut slabs, fifteen to seventeen feet long, of uneven thickness, but we managed to mastermind them (Kreskin-like) into agreement.

We used the offcuts with metal inlay for the chef's counter. Skins from the yellow-painted hops floor joists graced the face of the bar. The tabletops were crafted from Foppiano wine tank wood and bracketed with angle iron.

Since cedar shiplap from an Idaho grain shed dressed the front, we designed a metal SOUTHPAW BBQ sign with rusty corrugated and flat stock. Our master metalsmith did us proud with that and the outdoor menu case.

"It was important for us to use recycled materials in creating Southpaw. We also wanted to create a warm, inviting atmosphere. Working with Heritage Salvage has been a phenomenal experience. Not only did they help us choose the best reclaimed wood for each aspect of our restaurant, they also helped us in our design process, and explained the story and origins behind all the wood. We love sharing the stories with our customers. I am so impressed by their creativity and the craftsmanship of their woodwork."
—Elizabeth Wells, co-owner, Southpaw BBQ

Old Herb

When we took down a barn out in West County, I would head out each morning to start the crew, but what I really wanted to do was have coffee with Old Herb, who was ninety-two. I would ask Herb how he was this morning, and he would say something like, "Well, I woke up . . . then I wiggled my toes . . . and then I looked down to see if they was wigglin' . . . and they was, so I said, 'Yeehaw!' and got outta bed to see another sunrise."

BLEACHER BOARD BOOGIE

Boards Reclaimed from Gymnasiums, Gum 'n' All

Bleacher boards are really fun to work with. Nothing quite like butt-rubbed bleachers for that polished look. Our first set of bleachers came from Oxnard High School. The bleachers were installed in the '50s, I think. First credit card invented, first TV broadcast, Ike is president, Jimmy Dean and James Dean are hot, rock 'n' roll begins, Esther Williams swims, Elvis gets drafted . . . apples cost twelve cents a pound and coffee eighty cents.

Next we got the bleachers from Sonoma Valley High School, Sequoia High School in Redwood City (where they had been sat upon by students such as Gordon Moore, later of Intel, and Ray Dolby), and then we moved on to Southern Illinois University Carbondale (ditto Duane Kuiper, Walt Frazier, Jim Belushi, and Dick Gregory). Most recently we played the five-card hand of getting bleachers from five schools in Kansas City, Kansas! These patina-ed, numbered, hand-carved, lettered beauties of clear fir have wandered far and wide in the Heritage Salvage world!

HOPMONK SONOMA

Dean Biersch wanted to start a Hopmonk Sonoma, so he just up and called me to come look at the building as it was. I sashayed around there with Dean and his contractor, the always amiable Jeff Mills, and we threw around a whole bunch of ideas. Dean removed a lot of pieces from the existing setup, then he and Kim Betzina (great designer: then girlfriend, now wife) came to the yard to pick though a new shipment of bleacher boards I had in the yard. (We often get called when schools are changing out their retractable gymnasium seating.)

Bleacher sets typically come in three sizes: the ⅝"×9" planks as the walkway, the 1"×9" as seating, and the ¾"×9" as the backs. What gets everyone excited is the seat numbers and row letters, and nobody made more creative use of same than these two!

Dean and Kim and Dean's nephew Troy came out

on a 100° day to pick through the boards (always much better to do this on cold days, as the gum doesn't stick so much). Row numbers, row letters, and lots of gum. They deserve major kudos for sticking it out (as it were), and we managed to find the centerpiece for the restaurant, all the tables, the bar, and the back bar.

Dean added what has now become one of our signatures, shiplap flooring. He first chose some of the leftover shiplap from Moscow, Idaho, to build his fence around the beer garden (and I tell you, Dean knows how to garden!). Then Dean and Kim picked the gnarliest of the Hops Warehouse shiplap and had it installed—and decided not to sand and finish. "We'll just let our clients finish it naturally!"

Hopmonk Sonoma opened the day before Thanksgiving (Dean's favorite day to open, and one of the biggest bar/restaurant days of the year), and it has been a smash hit ever since.

HOPMONK NOVATO

Here comes Dean again. This time around he was starting with the brand-new Southern Pacific Smokehouse in Novato, which had failed after just eight months. "Bug, I need you to come down here and figure out how we can take the polish off this joint!"

This was the first time we used our milled shiplap from grain elevators in one of Dean's creations. The cool thing about this milled shiplap is that it is reversible, and they wanted to keep the Novato floor a little lighter, so they used some boards on the newly milled side, and alternated both sides and sizes. The first thing we did (of course) was to install 4,000

square feet of shiplap flooring. The next thing was to incorporate some bleacher boards into the bar, but we went a different direction with some Chicago-style standing metal bar tables, a mid-height pair of community tables, and some metal accents on the shelves and back bar.

Then the beer gardens. Beer gardening, in every sense of the word, is one of my favorite kinds of gardening, and Dean is the Ace of Gardeners. Hopmonk Novato has been brought up to five-star beer garden quality with a stage, chicken roosts as beer lounges, slab tables and picnic tables, and all the beer that's fit to garden.

TAVERN + BEER GARDEN

PARK

YOU'RE INVITED: HERITAGE HOPS & SALVAGED MONKS
A BUG 'N' DEAN PRODUCTION

"Choosing to bring in reclaimed materials to create our space made perfect sense. All the unique touches, like row letters from university bleachers on our table and bar with the original plaques, and writing on the flooring, provide a warm feeling with stories to tell; authentic trumps all! It is great to be part of what Heritage Salvage does." —Dean Biersch

PARADIS NOW

The Paradis family approached us to do some remodeling at their fabulous old Pacific Heights gem, which they had just purchased for their growing family. On my first tour I was boggled by the woodwork. The builder was an architect in the late 1890s who used a different tree species theme for each room—curly redwood paneling and rafters in the great room, tiger oak in the dining room, and the door that separates them is curly redwood on one side and tiger oak on the other. We remodeled the attic, which was previously a games room, into an upstairs master bedroom. All the closets and offices were done in bleacher boards. We milled all the material and built custom cabinets, shelving, desks, wardrobes et al.

We also made a magnificent 52"×12' valley oak table that we had to fly in through the third-floor window. We had to separate the top from the trestle base and fly it in at an angle through the huge double-hung window. As it turned out, the missus never warmed to the house, and we flew it back out the window in May 2013 and sent it on its way to Kenwood, although for such a massive table, it was a long flight!

GATHERING THYME

Gathering Thyme in San Anselmo ordered bleacher boards that encompassed close to a hundred lineal feet of shelving, approximately seven feet high with eight shelves and a cabinet under each one. The results were most spectacular, the best use of refinished bleacher boards yet. Dan Ford and Ron Estill championed this one.

HI TOPS SPORTS BAR

I met Steve Woodward when George Snyder's first article came out in the *San Francisco Chronicle*. John Wagner was still holding court at the venerable Union Hotel in Occidental, and Steve was in the bar holding the paper, asking John how he might meet me. That was in 2004, and since then Steve has become a best friend, a collaborator, my bee teacher, Il Postino (a collector of rustic posts), and now our head appraiser and deconstructionist, among other things. You have and will read Steve's name a few times in this tome.

In 2012, Steve's son Jesse said he was building the first gay sports bar in the city. I was stunned. "You mean nobody has built a gay sports bar in San Francisco in all these years?" Jesse and his partners all came out to the yard to choose their wood. At first they were looking for a basketball floor or some such thing (more on the basketball connection later). I convinced them that bleacher boards from Kansas City, Kansas, were the way to go (it was what we had at the time).

They came out on a wonderful Saturday afternoon and picked and chose, and were well rewarded for

diligence. After the grand treasure hunt through 11,000 board feet of bleacher boards, they emerged victorious with pieces that had numbers, letters, green stripes, and/or student carvings, and built themselves quite a stack.

We then proceeded to make them a variety of beautiful tables, bar tables, and drink rails with the wood. They used the bleachers as accents, wall treatments, and what-have-yous! They chose some ash flooring we had for a huge glue-up bar that our own Mike Obrien made into a spectacular twenty-eight-foot bar top. More things than the Pride parade have stopped traffic on Market Street, and getting the bar top off the truck in one piece was one of them!

Needless to say, the Hi Tops sports bar is a smash hit. They appeared in *Sports Illustrated*. Of course, at the time the Giants just won the World Series, the 49ers were one pass away from winning the Super Bowl, and the Warriors made it to the playoffs.

Speaking of the Warriors, one of their owners is gay and has become friends with Jesse, and Jesse is on the board concerned with relocating the Golden State Warriors to the City. Brilliant!

OFF THE WALL

PISMO'S COASTAL GRILL

Super chef David Fansler came to the yard to buy an eclectic selection of materials for Pismo's Coastal Grill in Fresno; I was a bit incredulous. We made some tables for him and supplied him with a downright disparate combination of materials.

But David is one of the ultimate professionals in design-and-build for restaurants. When I made it to Fresno to view the finished product, I was astounded: a beautiful medley of materials in a great layout with an incredible menu. The only restaurant in Fresno with a fish market, concentrating on fresh seafood, it did seven million in business last year. The man knows his market. Now David is working on a Westwood BBQ and Spice Company.

WESTWOOD BBQ AND SPICE CO.

David was considering taking over the lease of a Claimjumpers restaurant that failed, a monolith of timbers and metal that needed to warm up—a lot. We decided on a semi-load of materials from Vinegar Tank skins to old Idaho shiplap and some beautiful

mortise and tenon 6'×6's from an early 1900s Eastern Washington barn. I am sure the place will be open by the time this book hits the rack.

MOMA

In 2008, Sam White from Chez Panisse approached me about a food-themed performance art gig he was doing at SFMOMA as part of OPENrestaurant. They were going to bring a whole spit-roasted calf—by bicycle!—through the streets of San Francisco and into the kitchen, where it would be carved and served with libations of an artsy sort, following a lecture on visual performance art by RoseLee Goldberg. It was to be a big event, and they wanted us to make tables to carve the beef on, so we made two honkin' tamarack slabs to put on metal bases, and a small plinth describing the origins of the materials. I asked Chris Cheek, our longtime woodworker, to accompany me, and he was tickled that something he made was going to be in SFMOMA. Chris has taught art at Analy High School for some twenty years, and we figure he has over 6,000 art students roaming the planet!

OPPOSITE LEFT TO RIGHT: *Westwood ceiling; SFMOMA;* **THIS PAGE:** *Pismo's (fish in Fresno??): HS accents from the view to the loo.*

BELLY

Young Pablo Scurto came over with his pop, Johnny Scurto, owner of Tres Hombres and restaurateur/entrepreneur of many places and gigs, and said he was going to take over Checkers Restaurant in Santa Rosa. I thought, "Cool, it will be fun to see how the kid manages to fly the nest and how much Johnny will bend." Well, after some sage advice, Johnny just got out of the way. Pablo and his partner, Gray Rollin (rock star chef and chef to the rock stars), asked if I would help design the place. Damn right, I said—it is part of my bliss to help people change a space with the materials we have available.

We discovered bricks behind the stucco, a floor beneath the lino and carpet, and some pieces to feature. Next we went to new, sleek rolling garage doors, and a beautiful thirty-foot chocolate heart bar that went in and out! Then we used old Ft. Baker jailhouse window guards to shape the sidewalk seating. They are doing mighty fine over there at Belly.

BARN IT ALL

The Best Barns and Structures Repurposed and Restored, and Some That Got Away

BEE HERE NOW

Honeybees are the only insects that make food for us. After listening to the amazing tales of many beekeepers, I was interested in getting a hive or two. One day, a wonderful gentleman named Yossi Shahar wandered into the yard looking for some particular 2x (2"thick) material. He seemed to be very particular about the exact material he needed, so I asked him what it was for. Yossi replied that it was for beehives and I replied, "I thought you only needed 1x material for hives."

"Well," he said, "these are biodynamically designed top-bar hives built more in the shape that the bees like to live in."

"And how do you know that?"

It seems that Yossi was a nuclear physicist who dedicated his smarts to studying bees for a while. These beautifully designed hives are now at Heritage Salvage Yard.

HOPMONK SEBASTOPOL

When I first met Dean Biersch, he walked the yard with me, looking for some fencing for Hopmonk Sebastopol. He decided it was too expensive, as he could buy it new for one-third the price, and asked if I had something else, as he did like the idea of being sustainable. He'd already used some reclaimed materials for his floors there. That night I wrote him an email telling him that in a progressive town like Sebastopol sustainability with local product was the bees' knees, even though it cost a little more. I had a pile of cool-looking siding from a fruit-drying co-op in Sebastopol and he bought it all. We haven't looked back since.

PETALUMA CITY HALL

During Brighter Planet's 350 Challenge in 2009, our good friends at Daily Acts organized a massive landscape makeover at Petaluma City Hall. This included removing lawn, mulching, building garden beds, rainwater catchment, and planting the beds. Heritage Salvage was more than happy to build massive beds of corrugated and used redwood decking. There must have been over a hundred volunteers to implement this grand plan. Between Petaluma Bounty, Rebuild Petaluma, and Daily Acts, the place was rockin'! At times I am unsure who runs City Hall, but that day we overran it! By the end of the day, the table was set, and I see veggies in there every year. Go Petaluma!

Poem

*The pleasing
state of a
saddle-backed
barn
Inherent within . . .
its inevitable yarn.
The builders of
same and
the wood that
can talk
will tell more
tales from her
new place on
the block!
A sway-backed barn
outlines a ridge
a rusty sign . . .
a covered bridge
a wooden peg
a hand-hewn beam
all these things . . .
repurposed dreams*

OPPOSITE: *A barn in Oregon I had to go back to photograph;* **ABOVE:** *The barn that starred in our* Trash 2 Treasure *video;* **BELOW:** *Future yard by Chris Cheek.*

WELCOME to PETALUMA

FORMSHLAG BARN

After we had "Deakin-structed" a barn in Penngrove on Formshlag Lane, some folks building a new house were looking for a barn door as an art piece for their great room. At the time I was running the yard on this idyllic five-acre "Ag"(ricultural) property on Petersen Lane in West Petaluma. They missed a couple of appointments and raised my ire, but at long last they showed up in a giant yellow Humvee, and I proceeded to show them my favorite door. I charged them $1,500 and another handful of moolah to clean and clear-coat it with seven coats of lacquer. When they asked if I knew where it was from, it turned out they were building a home directly across the street from the site of the barn! Ah, the irony!

MOSHIN VINEYARDS

Our relationship began when I met Amber Cartwright in Occidental; she was one of my favorite bartenders. Amber married Rick Moshin, a math professor from San Jose State, who had realized his passion and turned winemaker . . . nice segue, Rick!

Rick had come out to Heritage Salvage when it was just one man in a chicken barn on some Ag property in Petaluma. We traded wine and a little money for wood, and so began a beautiful relationship. Between trading tables for barrels, attending a lot of our functions, and being ever generous with their bottles, Rick and Amber are as delightful as their wine . . . or vice versa! Moshin Vineyards is an engaging oasis out on Westside Road in Healdsburg, with some very fetching offerings.

FLORA GRUBB

Flora came out to look for materials and various pieces for her new venture, an upscale garden center in Bayview-Hunters Point, a low-rent district in San Francisco. I asked her, "Upscale? Bayview? Are you nuts?" Well, if you go by Flora Grubb Gardens today, you will see that she was not!

When she and her honey, Kevin Smith, a skilled builder, welder, and artist, were starting the project from the ground up, Flora walked around the 'hood, gave some street kids a few bucks, introduced herself, and asked if they would watch her new spot for her.

These days Flora Grubb Gardens is a paragon of change, an oasis in the fields of Bayview, and a learning center for many. We made a couple of furniture pieces, and Kevin did a lot of the creative installation of barnwood and corrugated metal on the diagonal.

There are so many life lessons and elegant approaches I have learned from the many clients-slash-friends of Heritage Salvage. Sustainability carries with it so many blends of spirit, empathy, community, camaraderie, earth essence, and sensibility . . . to have chosen this path is a blessing I keep receiving over and over.

LEVI STRAUSS AND Q3

The Quakers had just purchased the old Levi Strauss building in San Francisco and needed to do an earthquake retrofit before they could open it as a Friends school. Hence Q3. It was the first remodel after the 1906 'quake (Levi Strauss said we can't very well rebuild a city without our work jeans), and now the Quakers were doing an earth-Quake retrofit!

The first person I sold this wood to was looking for a mantelpiece with his wife. After looking at many possibilities, I lifted the tarp off the newly arrived pile and pointed at a 3×12 circle-sawn old-redwood floor joist, mentioning how cool it was that they were from the old Levi Strauss building in the city. His wife gasped and said, "My god, he worked for Levi Strauss for thirty-five years!"

They bought one of the 3×12s.

BOB WITHINGTON

Bob called Heritage to tell us he had a couple chicken barns to dismantle; we had no idea that we were going to meet such a raconteur—and an amazingly selfless human to boot. Here is Bob in advanced stages of cancer and his wife has Parkinson's, and he is making sure he cleans up his property before he goes. Our deconstructionist and genuine good guy Steve Woodward took care of Bob and all the clean-up, way above and beyond the call of duty. Here you see Steve's estimate on the material in the barn and how neatly they stack dumpsters to save fees. I made a video of Bob to pass on to his family, although he was such a joy to be with and such a great storyteller I often forgot to roll the camera.

Top: *Steve Woodward's notes on deconstruction;* **Above:** *Steve;* **Below:** *Non-repurposable wood stacks.*

RIGHT AND BELOW: *Since Louisiana is divvied up into parishes not counties, I always imagined this New Orleans anecdote being told in an old church and voila, you have an anecdote I heard in an elevator in the Parish of New Orleans sitting by a beautiful old church I photographed and fell in love with in Idaho!*

WILLOWS, CALIFORNIA

One stormy day in January 2007 I got a call from one Jason, a young man living in Willows, California. He said that his grandmother had told him he should take the old barn down and sell the wood before it fell down. I asked him to take a couple pictures and email them; I would give him an estimate of the value of the wood. He and his girlfriend took a few photos and went into the house to send them, when the storm kicked it up a notch, and they heard a horrendous crunching sound.

The photos seen here are the before and after. I stopped in Willows, inspected the leftovers, and purchased some of the material.

Karen, my GM, still works on the table we made from the last of the Willows circle-sawn fir rafters.

CREEKSIDE BARN RECYCLING COMPANY

When I was looking for a warehouse in Crestline, Ohio, for Brad Marquart and his Creekside Barn Recycling Company to work out of, I was pointed to the old mill by Joe Dzugan. The next thing I know is I bought an 1869 grain mill for $18,000, which we repurposed and spread around the countryside. I still own four lots on the railroad tracks and a small city street that I would like to name Reclamation Road. I took this shot of the mill while I was waiting for the train to pass, and posted it on Facebook. My friend Ricky Watts, an illustrator and painter, exclaimed, "That is a famous graffiti artist on that car; can you send it to me in high res?" I also got to know the wonderful Dzugan clan and discovered their oasis just outside Crestline. If you embrace the people you meet as family then that is who they become!

TOP: *Sketch by Chris Cheek;*
BELOW: *Darrin Eichhorn mills around;*
BOTTOM: *Joe Dzugan's playground;*
OPPOSITE TOP: *Graffiti on the track,*
Grain mill at the back;
OPPOSITE BOTTOM: *Grain mill.*

STRAUS FAMILY CREAMERY

Albert Straus is a sincere delight. When I first interviewed him on my KRSH radio show, he told me this engaging story of his mother. Shortly after Albert's mom read Rachel Carson's *Silent Spring*, she decided to ban all pesticides, etc., from the dairy. She also became a champion for the cause and sat on the board of many environmental groups. Every time the phone rang Albert's dad would call out, "Honey, it's for you! It's the environment calling!"

Straus has kept up the sustainable dairy farming ever since, and when they moved into the new warehouse offices in Petaluma, Albert wanted a place in there to feel like home, so they commissioned Heritage Salvage to build a milk bar. The stools are made from vintage metal milk cans. We whitewashed original barn siding. Old fence pickets, granary flooring, rusty corrugated caps; we put a picture of one of their dairy cows back in an old-time divided light window, and it's the coolest place for frozen yogurt in town—but you need to be a client.

We also built them a trade show booth a few years back, which everyone began to emulate. It came concomitant with milk-painted barnboard, corrugated-eyebrow classic redwood railing, and a beautiful folding fir floor, which we are currently expanding to a 10'×20' booth. Clover Stornetta has also ordered one after seeing Straus's at the trade show.

OPPOSITE: *Liz Scatena w/ "Bessie" in the trade show booth;* **LEFT:** *Athena as the Straus Mouse;* **RIGHT:** *Milk bar;* **BELOW:** *Rich Martin bartends at daughter's birthday at the Milk Bar.*

THE LADIES OF THE LONG TABLE

Susan Villa, a delightful, very involved Englishwoman in Petaluma, has been a fellow expatriate of a very special kind. We first met when she was president of the Petaluma Historical Library Association. Susan invited me to come speak at the Library Museum about reusing, reclaiming, and repurposing the vast collection of chicken barns and barns in general in Sonoma County. That was my first public speaking gig with Heritage Salvage; my, how we have grown!

Somewhere along the way Susan and I discovered we were brother and sister from a different set of parents. She is an inspiring asset with oodles of dry Brit wit to keep us rolling!

Susan decided she wanted a long dining table, serving counter, and mantelpiece out of matching material, and we went to the beautiful clear-fir vinegar-tank staves from Manzana Products in Graton. The tanks, redolent of apple cider vinegar, had to be dried and aired for a couple of years before we could use them. The striations of vinegar stain, aged fir, and patina-ed exterior lent a multilayered look to an elegant yet "skookum" (well-built) table. The 50,000-gallon tank in question was once pumped out to put out a huge fire at Manzana after the waterlines failed. I could just imagine the scent of a gourmet chef's burning vinegar drifting far on the flames!

Susan, the Long Table, and her Sisters of the Long Table still have many themed events around same.

West County Gazette 6/07

Tankin' it at Manzana

By Michael "Bug" Deakin

In the ever-changing "what's next" world of Heritage Salvage I had the extreme pleasure this month to get to know Dick Norton and Mark Fitzgerald at Manzana Family in Graton . . . what a breath of fresh air for apple cider vinegar), they and their business are! You've certainly caught the scent of pressed apples and vinegar if you haven't seen them in Graton during apple season.

The company has been in the same family since it's inception in the 1920's. Mr. and Mrs. Oehlmann started it as the Oehlmann Evaporator, a fruit drying facility. In 1945 they changed the name to Manzana as they must have had a premonition that Graton would one day have the first hiring hall for our amigos from across the border!

Now there are two grandchildren, Suzi Kaido, President, and Dick Norton, Treasurer, and three great grandchildren, Kim Kaido-Alvarez, Kristi Pierson, and Patrick Norton actively involved. The whole gang is as friendly as all-get-out, and they are the last surviving pioneer apple processor in the area. Why, if it wasn't for them, we'd have to rename Gravenstein Highway the Cabernet Highway. Thank goodness we still have the apple blossoms and all the benefits they bring . . . the bee population, the apples, sensible land usage, and apple juice, applesauce and cider vinegar galore. Long live the apple orchard!

We are soon going to take down some redwood wine tanks in the south bay. The patina of red wine soaked through the tank wood is brilliant. I am also going to see a redwood water tank on the coast soon . . . purported to be thirty feet tall.

And . . . speaking of water tanks, we are constantly reminded of our gross mismanagement of our water systems. It seems that our intrepid Gazette and the Russian River Monthly are always filled with articles about our water situation. I just finished a book on the War of 1812 and a year after the Battle

You can support this wonderful local company by checking out their organic and natural products found at most local stores under their brands, such as Safeway, Whole Foods, Trader Joes and Andy's Produce. They also have their own brand, North Coast Applesauce at Whole Foods. And don't forget, whenever you see Gravenstein Applesauce and Apple Juice, you know it came from Sebastopol Apples and Manzana Products, Inc!

Then there was the tank! We removed a 100,000 gallon vinegar tank made of 3" thick fir. It was 16' tall and 32' in diameter. It would have made the coolest great room, cutting arched windows into the staves and a conical roof. I played a drum inside before we tackled the rotting roof and the acoustics were amazing. The floor would be the finest yurt floor you ever did see! They really built those tanks well. All the flooring and underpinnings on the vinegar tank still had their hand written assembly numbers on them.

of Tippecanoe the great Shawnee Chief Tecumseh said, "The long knives are our enemies. We gave them rivers of fish and they poisoned our fountains. We gave them forest clad mountains and valleys of game and in return what did they give our warriors and women? Rum and trinkets and a grave."

We live in this beautiful place on a fabulous continent of land. It is incumbent upon us to care for it all. The most erudite Chief Tecumseh met with W.H. Harrison, governor of Indiana Territory in 1810. The Governor talked of selling land.

"Sell land!" exclaimed Tecumseh. "Why not sell the air, the clouds, or the great sea? Did not the Great Spirit make them all for his children?"

As we all strive to embrace global cooling, remember that at Heritage Salvage, we endeavor to help you build green by re-using, re-purposing and reclaiming. Visit us at www.heritagesalvage.com or drop on by our fabulous yard in Petaluma. We are happy to help with creative, sustainable solutions to your building needs.

In 1948, Manzana Products Co. had a catastrophic fire. Employees attempted to put out the fires with cider vinegar, but the plant was damaged so severely that it had to be rebuilt. At this point the decision was made not to replace the kilns. The business was changed to a cannery and fruit drying was discontinued.

SGT. KEN

Sgt. Ken Savano of the Petaluma Police Dept. has a sort of take-no-prisoners attitude when it comes to reclaiming, reusing, and repurposing our county's plethora of chicken barns. He made this dartboard from some Heritage Salvage scraps—but he had been born with a passion for the wood. In the middle of our early relationship came the great story of his then-wife Lisa and the prune trays for Harlan Estates.

As our relationship grew he revealed more of his roots, and we helped him deconstruct a relative's chicken barn; he is an incorrigible wood hoarder! Then it ends up he too has a chicken barn on his property, which has been repurposed as a wedding/event venue.

Ken was always stopping by the yard to see what worked. Top of his list were the classic six-light windows that were in all the chicken-barn kits. Then wooden gutters, an old flagpole, a slab for a bar top—and he just keeps going. I sold Ken a table way back when

HS was on Peterson Lane, and even loaned him the truck to take it home.

A month before Christmas I had gone down to the COTS (Committee on the Shelterless) Mary Isaak Center and asked if any of the folks wanted some seasonal employment. Eventually eight of them tried it out. The shortest stint was two hours and the second-longest tenure was five days. But the longest and greatest success was Scotty Johnson, who ended up working with us for over six months. We helped him get his son back; he got a job with the Sonoma Marin Fairgrounds, moved into an apartment, and moved forward with his life.

When I asked Scott to go with Ken Savano to deliver the table, he asked, "Do I get to sit in the front?"

I have watched the Sarge do a great job of policing Petaluma, keeping his passion for building with the original material, and becoming a good friend! I have the feeling he would love to take a road trip with HS, but he may have to check with his wife, Kat.

Now K2 Ranch is ready to roll
Loyal dog Olive on patrol
Chicken barn and nesting box
Refectory table—if it could talk!

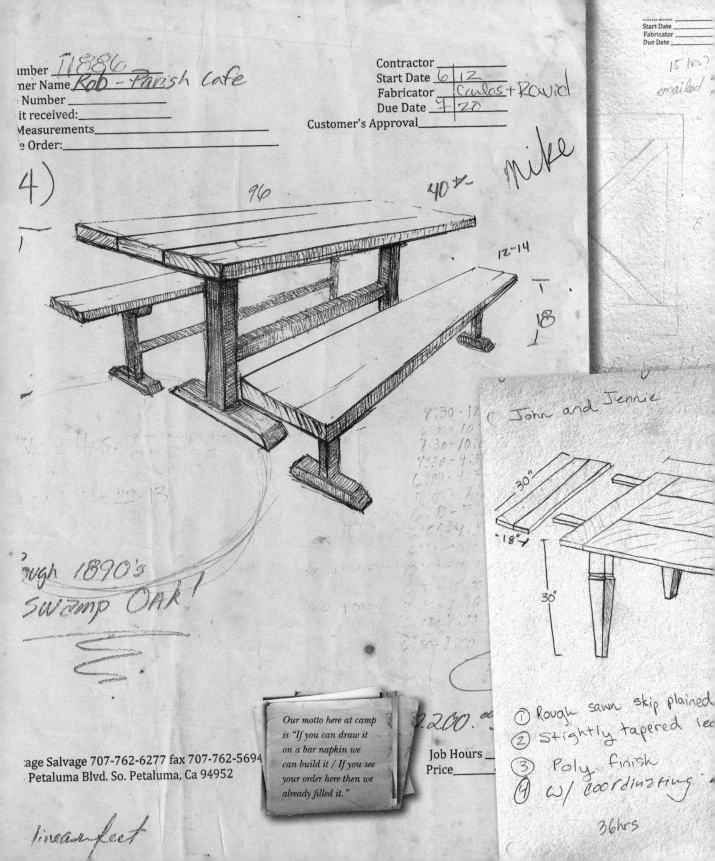

umber II886
ner Name Rob - Parish Cafe
Number _____
it received: _____
Measurements _____
e Order: _____

Contractor _____
Start Date 6 | 12
Fabricator Carlos + Rowid
Due Date 7 | 20
Customer's Approval _____

4)

96   40"   Mike

12-14

18

nike

through 1890's
swamp Oak!

John and Jennie

30"

~18"

30"

① Rough sawn skip plained
② slightly tapered leg
③ Poly finish
④ w/ coordinating

36hrs

age Salvage 707-762-6277 fax 707-762-5694
Petaluma Blvd. So. Petaluma, Ca 94952

Our motto here at camp is "If you can draw it on a bar napkin we can build it / If you see your order here then we already filled it."

2200. oo

Job Hours _____
Price _____

linear feet

(2)

5

6

80"

6

Slab Doors
Redwood
to match Ta
1¾ Thick
louvered lower
sho??? panel
OSMO Finis

"PAM'S SMOKEHOUSE"

TIN ROOF

OPEN for air flow

12"

12"

17"

12"

All 5 sides
need
protection
from weather
84"

screen
Door
24"

This netting
for bugs can
be tacked over
door opening

NO DOOR
(NEED lots
of air flow)

4'

At

4'

For   510 - E

CUSTOMIZE YOUR SPACE
SEPARATORS W/ RARE EARTH
MAGNETS

MAGNET   METAL
SHELF   PLANTER

METAL
CAR

feather 6
May 23, 201?

6-2013

ADAM

Note: please cut 6" off left side
and 7⅞" off Right side
center beam to Legs   — 7⅜

6

30½"

30½

36½"   13"   138"   12¾"   37⅞"   21

8"   8"   1½"   8"

od top
ed at the

— that
tucks u

3,028.⁰⁰

⁑ Pull + kiln Dry   — 13/8

⁕ Brush

⁕ Light sand (Raw)

⁕ Poly

3/12/2
3/26/20
Sent another

No splines
only fill cracks No large
voids

83"

17"

7"

¾"
25¼" to ??
of ??

84" inside
measurement

72" inside measurements

⁕ 6×6 Tamera K   3(71) #378
⁕ Black Acacia   Slabs #650
⁕ (2 x 10) Tamerak #420

LAB02.
28 hrs @ 95⁰⁰
$1,760.00

THE LOCALS

NATIVE AMERICANS

INDIGENOUS WISDOM

From my early beginnings in the Kootenays to meeting Chief Dan George to exploring and discovering the amazing art and ways of the First Nation Peoples of Canada, I have always admired and respected the indigenous peoples. Just the fact that Canada chooses to call them First Nation Peoples, as they should be called, speaks volumes of respect. I often wonder why Columbus is referred to as having "discovered" America when there were millions living here at the time. What would have happened if they had hung out a NO TRESPASSING sign?

My relationship with the people of local roots has always been a joy, a spiritual gleaning as it were. From a childhood fascination with birch bark and its potential as watercraft to the time I have spent with the locals, I have learned so much!

MIWOK PARADE FLOAT

When the theme of the annual Butter and Egg parade for 2008 was announced as the 150th birthday of Petaluma, I decided to call it the 1500th birthday instead, and invited the Miwoks from the Graton Rancheria to participate with me on a float. The parade committee was a little reticent to approve the idea, until I reminded them that the Miwoks had actually founded Petaluma probably more like 10,000 years ago.

(There is controversy on the meaning of the city's name. Some say it's a transliteration of the name of the original Coast Miwok village, *Péta Lúuma*, which means "the backside of the hill," although Graton Rancheria matriarch Gloria Armstrong told me it meant "place of the sloping ridges," and the Chamber of Commerce thinks it's more like "flat back.")

At one unfortunate point in Petaluma's history there was actually a bounty offered on the local natives, and the Miwok population was decimated. Once I was given the go-ahead for my float design, I had Chris Cheek, our art teacher, draw up a Miwok kotcha (a conical home covered with redwood bark) and a tule boat, and I sent it to Lorelle Ross, vice chair of Graton Rancheria, to get their blessing. *OMG*, came back the email, *is that my old art teacher who signed these?*

So a few weekends later we were joined by Gloria, her daughter Lorelle, Linda, and three other Miwoks, along with George Snyder, Ron Estill, and Chris Cheek from Heritage and Kate Weaver the weaver. I served smoked salmon for lunch on one of our showroom tables, and I told Gloria that typically, shortly after using a table, it sells! When she asked if I had any kids, I told her the story of Suzy, my daughter, whom I had not heard from yet. Gloria smiled and said, "She will find you very soon." The table sold three days later and my daughter found me three months later!

The resulting float, with two beautiful draft horses pulling her, was a treat, and an award-winner. Cheek also portrayed a very classic "pooper scooper." I was especially proud of representing the First Nation Peoples, and that my dear friend George Snyder rode on the float, standing behind Gloria Armstrong. Although I received a lot of flak for featuring the Graton Rancheria on our float while they were trying to get permission to open a casino in Rohnert Park, I stood behind my honoring of their First Nation status. The powers that be had promised that they would use a bunch of reclaimed building materials for the casino, which is now open, but alas, they never once returned my emails or phone calls.

CLOCKWISE FROM TOP: *the Matriarch; Ike and Spark; the Na Na's; native beauties in a Miwok kotcha; kotcha; sign; Linda in her regalia; George w/Gloria!* **OPPOSITE, LEFT TO RIGHT:** *Chief Dan, George Snyder, Kate Weaver.*

Happy 150th
Birthday
Molis Kenekkus
Liilek Siyenpo
Aayak hii
Peta-tuuma

Photos by KENT PORTER / The Press Democrat

Salmon Creek Middle School's Connor deJong, 13, counts the rings on a 370-year-old redwood slab Thursday in Occidental. The slab was cut from a tree uprooted during a winter storm on school property. DeJong and Lauren Janney, 13, were pinpointing and labeling historical dates in correlation to the rings on the trunk.

THE GIVING TREE

LEFT: *Merle Reuser starts reclaiming windfall;* ABOVE: *Andy Paul buys wood for his barn.*

L. FRANK

L. Frank (Manriquez) is a Tongva-Acjachemen artist, writer, tribal scholar, cartoonist, and indigenous language activist who lives and works in Santa Rosa, California. I asked her if she would come out to Salmon Creek School while we were dealing with "Windfalla," a massive windfall redwood on the beautiful acreage next to the school grounds. I wanted her to bless the tree and tell the students a little about how the Miwoks lived in and with the forest.

When I first met her I knew she was someone special, but as I got to know her I was more and more thrilled. It was magical in the forest, surrounded by trees and students all tuned in to the story and the singsong blessings of L.

When the Europeans first arrived in California, they were astounded at how park-like the forests were. That was because the indigenous peoples always burned off the undergrowth to facilitate the growth of their medicinal plants, and as a fire suppressant. (Today our forest fires rage through overgrown underbrush.)

Her blessing was spellbinding and her talk was riveting. "Windfalla" was ready to roll. We milled the tree and stacked and stickered the lumber on the school grounds, and Heritage Salvage sold the lumber, giving 85% of the gross back to the school.

A little later L called and asked that if I ever came across a log about two feet in diameter and ten inches long, would I let her know?

"Green or dry?"

"I want to make a practice canoe with the kids in my neighborhood."

About a month later I asked Art Glueck, who runs a tree service, about the trees they'd just taken down at the Camp Meeker Firehouse. Art and I went and bucked one about ten feet, with nary a knot, and Art said we'd just throw it on the heavy equipment truck and fly it over L's wall. Our plan until then had been, in L's words, to "Egyptian it through the front gate somehow." We took the log, given the pet name of "PC" (Practice Canoe), and his big rig, and I called L from outside the fence as the log was in the air. "Go to your back yard, L."

She came out and was, well, canoe-struck, and immediately started telling the story to her friend on the phone. "So I wished for a practice canoe and this huge redwood log came flying over the wall in my back yard . . ."

Since then L has amassed a consortium of canoe carvers from many different tribes. Last time I visited I asked her how many, and she said she had way lost count, but someone from Kazakhstan had just been there! In her yard were a redwood dugout canoe and a couple of traditional plank boats, all redolent of cedar shavings.

Each time a crew assembles at L's, she reminds them that Bug and the PC started this whole thing. L. Frank, I am proud to be the instigator of this growing collaboration, although I brought just a wee bit of tree, and you linked such a wide array of peoples around it.

CLOCKWISE FROM TOP: *w/Dune; w/Pam and Carol from Eyak Preservation Council; Art Glueck; L. Frank with the "PC"; L. Frank and me.*

Sawyer extraordinaire Merle Reuser & his 6' bar

Native artist & storyteller L. Frank blesses Windfalla with a traditional prayer

Merle slicing a burl

THE SALMON CREEK WINDFALL
STORY & CEREMONY

Heritage Salvage

has spearheaded a windfall operation at Salmon Creek School in Occidental, CA. A magnificent and young (200 years) redwood tree fell in a storm in 2003 and has since been blessed in a community ceremony, then milled, stacked, and stickered. We named her Windfalla.

Proceeds from the sale of the wood will benefit the school's programs in environmental education and sustainable forestry practices. There is aproximately 8,000 board feet of 1x12's and a very unique collection of cants & slabs all from one incredible tree!

The students counted 342 rings in this center slab !

Bug talkin' story with the students about sustainble forestry & reclaimed lumber

Half sawn piece ready for milling

1 x 12's fresh off the mill !

HERITAGE SALVAGE
Reclaimed Building Materials & Salvage Boutique

FESTIVALS

RIVERTOWN

Rivertown Revival, "The Greatest Slough on Earth," is a unique arts-based, annual al fresco community festival that celebrates the Petaluma River. It takes place at the David Yearsley River Heritage Center, a century-old barn I helped restore. Masterminded by Clementine Eco Events (Kelin Backman, Vannessa Hauswald, and Elizabeth Howland), it features all kinds of art—art boats, art performances, aerial acts, music, wandering sideshows, and crafts—all set in the wonderful world of steampunk Victoriana. Here's a tribute I wrote to Rivertown, which is the voiceover on a great video by Brickroom Studios in Petaluma:

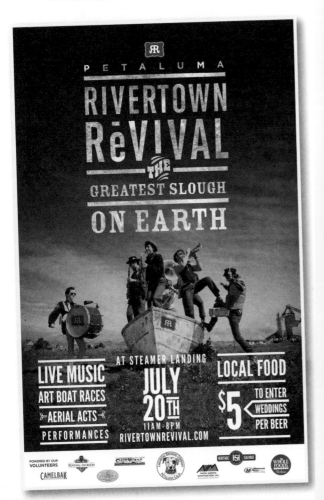

Rivertown . . . Revival, it's almost here!
as the seasonal burg of
Rivertown takes shape
the artisans and buskers
camp in nearby fields
a train whistles by unheeded as
the working boats ply the shores
the crinolined beauties sashay by
the river twirling their parasols
groups of carnival hawkers
dance lightheartedly
as the ambers of Lagunitas
bubble under the moon
ohhh . . . the anticipation of
tomorrow gets the river boys
flirting amongst the dancing debs
by the front porch

a giant chair ponders the river!

the Highway Poets arrive by Boets
as Rivertown Revives
the light fog lifts her morning veil
as Father Sun arrives

a special time on the mighty slough
with volunteers and hearty crew
8300 came and danced
and some . . . got married too

the music played on stages three,
a boat, the front porch, and a barn you see
the preacher proselytized in style
music playing all the while

art boats plied the river slough
swans, Pink Boobs, and rainbows too
wheeled contraptions, ordered chaos
matters not who won and lost

a sculpture garden and teeny town
a special section to kid around
handcar regatta and robots too
a kaleidoscope of things to do

music, music, rhythmic stomp
Dirtfloor, Huckle, Crux, and Swamp
Smokehouse, Hubub . . . Shovelman
Highway Poets and Jugtown Band

Radio KRSH and Clementine
Lions, Tigers and Hair of Thine
Heritage Salvage and Lucky Star
Friends of the River . . . where we are!

sponsors all, we thank you more
Natal, Jerico, Boho . . . Encore
Minuteman, Nomad and Paige Out West
All you sponsors are the best

a Green event of fine proportion
trapeze artists in contortion
walk in, boat in . . . bicycle valet
costumes, oddities and water ballet

our Facebook page is full of love
over 8,000 people and not a shove
if you missed the show this year
next year will bring even more to cheer

the day turned in timeless script
a roaring success, a throwback trip
to volunteers we tip our cap
next year what shall be on tap?

CLOCKWISE FROM TOP: *33-foot party boat; Chairman of the Board and the Board of the Chair; the fair; the fair; the wedding arch; art boats; married first were Lindsey and John; Oona and Ri with Shane so Schlick; Chris No Hell; front porch of stage.*

CLOCKWISE SPIRAL FROM TOP: *Pink Boobs; Bluejacket; the Clementine Trio: Vanessa, Elizabeth, and Kelin; Briana dancin' with Katie and her sis; Nettie on trapeze; Oona insists; Savannah and Oona do the Titanic thing; Green Mary recycled everything; Nettie on a trapeze; art boat; me.*

HIGHWAY POETS

I would be remiss if I did not mention my good friend, collaborator, videographer, singer, songwriter, and all around amazing young human, Sebastian Nau. I started a relationship with "C-Bass" and this talented group of musicians during the Pyramid Party on 10/10/10. The band was then known as Hillside Fire, and they volunteered, as they always do, to play for our fundraiser for Danny Cox, who had been paralyzed in a diving accident . . . swim in peace, young Danny! Since then we have traveled many trails, and I am the richer for it! Highway Poets—Taylor James Schroder, Shane Schlick, and Travis James—my hat's off to you! Sebastian wrote a haunting tune, "Calling," for our Plastic Is Drastic campaign and he put my song "Empty Denim" to music.

CALIFORNIA LEGISLATURE

Assembly

CERTIFICATE OF RECOGNITION

HERITAGE SALVAGE

Sustainable Business Award

In recognition of your outstanding business practices incorporating the highest form of sustainability into your daily operations. Heritage Salvage's use of 100% recycled wood products effectively diverts materials from our landfills, preserving our treasured natural resources while providing top-quality products for the community. Your continuous environmental awareness is a model of sustainable business practices in Sonoma County.

THANK YOU AND CONGRATULATIONS!

Jared Huffman, Assemblymember, 6th District

April 2007

BOTTOM: *Shabby-chic Chris Cross knows how to shop;* **OPPOSITE:** *Gabby La La plays the accordion on our award-winning Butter & Eggs float.*

TO SAN FRANCISCO 38.34 ML.

PET
ELE

COMMUNITY ORGANIZATION

ACTIVISM IS PATRIOTISM

I first read Rachel Carson's *Silent Spring* in the summer of 1967 while working in a logging camp. It provoked hours/days/months/years/decades of thought for many of us, and is credited with helping to start the environmental movement. Public reaction to the book was the first time we saw Monsanto step up its war against anything disputing the Monsanto way!

Terri Swearingen was a nurse awarded the Goldman Environmental Prize in 1997 for organizing protests against Waste Technologies Industries' toxic waste incinerator in the Appalachian town of East Liverpool, Ohio. Her efforts influenced stricter nationwide limits for heavy metals and dioxin emissions from waste incinerators.

"Activism consists of efforts to promote, impede, or direct social, political, economic, or environmental change. Activism can take a wide range of forms: writing letters to newspapers or politicians; political campaigning; economic activism such as boycotts or preferentially patronizing businesses; rallies; street marches; strikes; sit-ins and hunger strikes." That is Wikipedia's definition of activism (thanks, guys). It can be implemented by doing those things you deem will make a difference. My idea of the ultimate activist is one who practices what they preach and shows the way by active involvement. You can have your Preach Pie and eat it too!

The more I shared the strength of "sustainable en-thusiasm," the more I realized positive demonstration was garnering results. I began morphing an original idea into a future vision.

THE HERITAGE SALVAGE TEAM

Heritage Salvage is so much greater than the sum of its parts. While I have regaled you with stories of some of the people and the buildings that have meandered through my life and the life of Heritage, I have not mentioned the main reason why we are so successful: I prefer to run my business as we were a family. That of course implies that it occasionally is dysfunctional, and with a delightful melding of different people from different backgrounds, it is! But the credit for the ultimate success of Heritage Salvage lies in the hearts and hands of the people who make

up the TEAM. The members of the team that make Heritage Salvage rock are here in full color . . . and colorful they all are . . . these wonderful people are the heart and soul of Heritage Salvage!

PETALUMA

I am fortunate to live in the wonderful town of Petaluma, which has a social infrastructure of amazing entities dedicated to enriching the community by their daily acts. Trathen Heckman, founder and executive director of **Daily Acts** (dailyacts.org), lives and teaches the mantra "Because every choice matters!"

Through creating media, initiating and sharing sustainability models, cultivating community networks and providing hands-on education, we empower citizens, strengthen leaders, and grow community self-reliance. Daily Acts fulfills a critical role in promoting positive examples to inspire vision, hope, and action. Its work is grounded in the principle that simple, mindful choices significantly enrich our lives and world. Citizens and leaders easily become overwhelmed by the diversity and scale of ecological and social crises. By highlighting amazing people and efforts that demonstrate sustainability, we share the powerful relationships, skills, and tools needed for healthy lives and a resilient world. We support sustainability pioneers, empower emerging leaders to share their stories and enable engaged citizens to make bold changes for care of self, people, and planet.

Next, I wander down the boulevard to 55 Shasta Ave., where the flagship farm of **Petaluma Bounty** (petalumabounty.org) creates a sustainable food system with healthy and fresh food for everyone!

Formed in 2006 with initial funding from the Hub of Petaluma Foundation, Petaluma Bounty is a community-based nonprofit that helps folks grow their own food, redistribute surplus food, and provide affordable fresh food to low-income families and seniors. I really like their version of Bounty Hunters: the gleaners who pick fruit and vegetables that other folks have too much of or will not get to picking.

Another outstanding member of the social structure that supports this community is **COTS**, the Committee on the Shelterless (cots-homeless.org). Their powerful, award-winning blend of nurturing and structure has helped thousands get back under a roof of their own

"Only within the moment of time represented by the present century has one species—man—acquired significant power to alter the nature of the world."
—Rachel Carson, *Silent Spring*, 1962

"We are living on the planet as if we have another one to go to."
—Terry Swearingen

CLOCKWISE FROM TOP:
Creek in Idaho; dams on the river; Desolation Peak; home under a rainbow; furniture from Red Tails *movie set.*

and rebuild their lives. They provide almost 350 beds every night. Their Petaluma Kitchen serves over 124,000 meals a year and delivers over 750,000 pounds of food annually.

Petaluma People Services Center (petalumapeople. org) is our neighbor across the street. PPSC is dedicated to improving the social and economic health of our community by providing programs that strengthen the dignity and self-sufficiency of the individual. Their goal is to reduce poverty, physical and mental abuse, chemical dependence, violence, ignorance, isolation, and mental illness among children, adults, families, and seniors. They deal with over ten thousand people a year! Recently, Petaluma Bounty moved under their umbrella.

My message is that *you can make a difference.* Everything you do makes a difference. You can generate the snowball effect by sharing an idea with friends and getting their assistance. The viral effect of how you can grow an idea is exponentially commensurate with how many people you add to the chain.

A case in point: In 2010 I became horrified at the extent of the great plastic gyres (vortices) we have created in our oceans. I started a campaign on my radio show, enlisted the help of radio station KRSH, and then Vesta Copestakes jumped in with the *Sonoma County Gazette.* Sebastian Nau, leader of the band Hillside Fire, got inspired and wrote our great anthem, "Calling." (You can hear it on their CD *Welcome Home.*) The whole exercise cost me about $15,000 but I got some of it back from the gate at the "Hillside Fire/Plastic is Drastic" show at Petaluma's Mystic Theater.

Now here's where it gets really good. Lagunitas Brewing Company, the brewery that keeps on giving, decided they liked the idea of beer festivals using stainless steel beer mugs. So far, they've printed 13,000 of them, all with my website and the **Plastic Is Drastic** logo. Their mascot dog says this is "getting rid of plastic one beer at a time." Now that is more than payback!

I want to touch on another pet peeve: the disintegration of our heirloom seed stock and the attempts by the giant Monsanto to control the world's food supply by using GMO seeds to feed the world. Genetically engineered seed is designed to require that farmers buy new seed every season. Here we have

Gere Gettle, the consummate seedsman, and our own **Petaluma Seed Bank**, which are working on inspiring people to collect and grow using heirloom seeds.

In India, for example, farmers nurtured their heirloom seeds, always collecting enough from the year's crop to plant next year's crop. Now that Monsanto has foisted GMO seeds on a subcontinent where 60% of the population farms, farmers can see no way to make a living. This deplorable practice has so affected the country's food supply that more than 17,600 farmers killed themselves in 2009. "Suicide seed," as they call it, was responsible for the death of a farmer in India every half hour that year!

Reclamation Road has a plan for this in the USA, as we take back the countryside one small town at a time. If we resuscitate our small towns by planting organic gardens with heirloom seeds, harvesting the seeds, and continuing the cycle, we become activists of the first order. By the small act of letting a few carrots go to seed, you can save the whole carrot patch.

The more you think about it, the more you realize we are growing so far apart: apart from the land, from each other, from what matters, from real dialogue with our fellow beings, too often separated by a two-dimensional screen of a four-dimensional reality!

Another genius of alternative building is the publisher and general delight known as **Lloyd Kahn**. He published *Shelter* in 1973, and has since published volumes on alternative building styles from all around the planet! I recently filmed a great video at Lloyd's cool complex on the California coast for *Reclamation Road* with his Lloydness; he inspires!

My relationship with **Merle Reuser** started many moons ago. He owned a portable sawmill, a very sweet disposition, and a yard full of reclaimed trees that he had milled and slabbed. He fit right in with Heritage Salvage. Merle has since passed his sawmill on to Shawn Gavin, another sweet human being, and we have worked with Shawn for a few years now. Merle has since gone on to follow his passion, hence the handle, the Daffodil Man. In memory of a longtime friend, mentor, and grandmother-figure, Margaret Adams, Merle wants to make Sonoma County the Daffodil Capital of the world.

TODAY'S spotlight

Michael "Bug" Deakin with stack of redwood flooring

Salvaging the Heritage of Old Wood

BY MICHAEL KRAWCZAK

Michael "Bug" Deakin still remembers the first house he ever built and lived in, back in 1967.

Throughout a long and varied subsequent career, using skills he learned from his dad, Deakin has remained in the periphery of the building industry, including a stint spent working on sets in the film industry in Los Angeles.

Along the way, he became driven by the art and rewards of repurposing, reusing, and recycling building materials as a way of life; a practice he says creates, "sustainable enthusiasm".

"If we are enthusiastic about that which

> **"To love what you are doing is one of the greatest assets in the world."**
>
> *–Michael "Bug" Deakin*

we do, we will never feel like work is work," he said. "To love what you are doing is one of the greatest assets in the world."

Today, Heritage Salvage, Deakin's five-year-old business on the shores of the Petaluma River, embodies those principles by rescuing old wood headed to landfills and reusing it for furniture and construction projects where people want an antique look.

"A big part of what I'm about is to salvage the heritage of what I'm about to take down," Deakin described. "It's how we got the name."

An example is the time a man passed up a higher offer to sell his six 14' redwood columns to Deakin.

"He discovered that I cared so much," said Deakin. "I wanted to know how they got there – the heritage."

Deakin photographs structures before tearing them down. The recent completion of a new barn constructed from old wood included a presentation to the new owner of one of those pre-teardown photographs in a frame built from the original wood.

This guiding construction philosophy led Deakin to incorporate his own name into a new word that describes a service offered by Heritage Salvage: "Deakin-struction" - Removal of buildings with a heart and the panache for recycling.

Over the past two years, Heritage Salvage has supported an elementary school in nearby Occidental in a unique manner that underscores the company's commitment to conservation. During a 2003 storm, a 370-year-old, 165-ft tall, 9-ft di-

BIRDHOUSE - assorted recycled metal & wood, sliding mini barn door.

KITCHEN ISLAND -FOR NAPASTYLE CATALOG - redwood, fir, metal

BARNWOOD TABLE- Redwood barnwood top, fir legs from power pole arms.

WINERACK - Redwood barnwood , holds 60 cases of wine

WOODSTACKS- Some stacks at our yard on the Petaluma River.

ameter redwood was felled on the grounds of Salmon Creek School. In the ensuing project, called Spirit of Windfall, the tree was systematically milled into 1x12s and slabs; stacked, stickered, and air-dried; and is now being sold, with 85 percent of the proceeds supporting Salmon Creek's environmental education programs.

"I love turning kids on to this," said Deakin. Indeed, the Heritage Salvage web site proclaims, "We design with children for free, there will be a charge for adult input!"

Environmental activist Julia "Butterfly" Hill, who famously lived in a redwood for two years to stop loggers, has embraced Deakin's work, accompanying him to many local conservation events, including Salmon Creek School.

All items for sale in Heritage Salvage's 1,400-square-foot showroom are one-of-a-kind or can be custom ordered. At any time, Deakin may tell his crew of seven woodworkers, "This week is 'Let the wood talk to you week.' Build it and we'll put it in the showroom," or "For the next three

days, make any birdhouse that tickles your fancy".

"Most of us consider ourselves artists," said Deakin. "I find every piece of wood I look at a work of art".

Heritage Salvage is located at 1473 Petaluma Boulevard South, Petaluma, Calif. 94952. Contact by telephone at 707-762-6277 or online at www.heritagesalvage.com. Business hours are Monday through Friday, 9 a.m. to 4 p.m. and Saturdays, 10 a.m. to 3 p.m.; closed Sundays.

The Band! **SPIRALING CLOCKWISE FROM TOP:** *Mike O'Brien on cribwall; Reggie Diaz on brushes; Heather "Just Jokin'" Gallagher on stacks; Tresea Helbing on phones; Bandleader Karen Helms; Dave Rawson on steel; Chris "Cup" Raby on chainsaw; Hilary La Porte on duster; Adam Provencher on the edge; Ron "Chef" Estill on putty; Bridgit Lee on smiles;* **OPPOSITE BOTTOM LEFT TO RIGHT:** *Adam, Chris, Mike, Reggie; Chris Cheek on belt sander.*

HERITAGE
SALVAGE
.COM
-762-6277

WELCOME
to Petaluma!

CLOCKWISE FROM TOP: *Bus Shoppe fashion shoot, 2013; Daily Acts breakfast; Diane Patterson on Big Chair; and the iconic Petaluma Library Museum during the Parade.*

FREE PUBLIC LIBRARY

HERITAGE SALVAGE ~ REPURPOSING PETALUMA'S HERITAGE ~
THIS FLOAT BUILT FROM RECLAIMED BUTTER & EGG BARNS!!

PETALUMA'S CHOICE

CLOCKWISE FROM TOP: *Fundraising at the Bounty; sign; Suzy Grady, hands in the dirt and her pen on a grant; t-shirts; Sebastian shoots while I talk story with Lloyd Kahn; Dachee, the pyramid; the mothership at HS.*

WELCOME

SHOWROOM
OFFICE

PLASTIC IS DRASTIC
Far off the oceans shore
there's an island that's no mans home
It's not a city but we all should know
Where it is cus it's bound to grow
we're callin
callin for you
HILLSIDE FIRE

The Krush 95.9

In Memory Of
Margaret Adams
May 16. 1896 – June 15. 2000

JOHN L. ALLEN
MEMORIAL FIELD

MLK

BERLINER MAUER 1961 - 1989

RECLAMATION ROAD

CLOCKWISE FROM TOP: *My old pal Merle Reuser and his daffodil quest; in his truck; the pyramid dressed for winter; Geralyn directs Trash 2 Treasure; Reclamation Road at the Berlin Wall; my brother Dennis with Janet . . . I miss him; Merle dances with daughter, Christine.*

I recently lost my younger brother Dennis to cancer. I had never really known him: he was eleven years my junior, so when I left home at seventeen, he was six. I spent three great days with him just before he left, and he urged me to reach out to family and friends.

There is nothing like a personal meeting, a greeting, a coffee, beer, or lunch with an old friend. Texting, e-mailing, Facebooking, or cell phone calls do not take the place of a good hug! I now try to call and see an old friend at least once a month.

The essence of *Reclamation Road* is about reinserting our social capital into small towns. To do this, engaging small-town America with a plan to repopulate our rural environment with quality living, we must make it attractive to those who would move there. By growing our own food, bartering skills with our neighbors, and taking ourselves off the grid, we can ensure a quality of life that will thrive with or without Washington. Our current economy—"of the Corporation, by the Corporation, and for the Corporation"—can take a back seat.

From what I have witnessed in the political arena lately, the system is broken. When the party not in power spends four years trying to scuttle all attempts by the party in power to make things work better in this country just so they can get elected, we have a problem. That problem will never go away voluntarily! That problem is systemic. The propagators are the ones in power.

We are the ones who need to fix our own lot! As I write these words we are witnessing a government shutdown that shows off the dysfunctionality of the very people who supposedly work for us!

Now is the time to occupy your place on the "I care" list. It is up to us to fix what is wrong.

I care about our future and the future of our fellow beings on the only Gaia we've got. The planet will be fine without us, but we don't stand a chance without her.

Don't let multinational corporations suppress your desire to express yourself. They may occupy the seats of power, but we still occupy the 99%.

There is a big move afoot to pasteurize any poignant presence of pressure on the status quo.

Practice Sustainable Enthusiasm. If you are enthusiastic about that which you do, it will never be work!

I love what I do.

TRASH TO TREASURE

When Diane Iles Parker and Geralyn Pezanoski (producer of the 2009 documentary *Mine*) approached me about shooting a short that embodied the soul of what Heritage Salvage was about, I got quite excited. They shot the whole thing in one day with a top-notch film crew, including Norman Bonney, DP, and Scott Compton on second camera. The finished product is by far our most watched video, and it still embodies the heart and sustainable enthusiasm that is Heritage Salvage.

RECLAMATION ROAD

THE ROAD LESS TAKEN

THE ROAD TO *RECLAMATION ROAD*

Heritage Salvage got her first big kick in the pants in 2004 from a soulful two-page article in the *San Francisco Chronicle*. George Snyder titled his great story "Barn Again."

When we talked about the story, he decided to spend a day on the road with me "barn spotting." During our ride I asked if he'd read the book *Blue Highways*.

"William Least Heat-Moon," he exclaimed, and we bonded further and began discussing a Barn Again tour.

On old-style pre-Google maps, blue highways were the small country roads traversing the state, while the red ones were the interstates. I had dreamed of riding across the country taking down collapsing barns, maybe fixing up some that needed gentle support.

The final morph that fashioned that Barn Again tour into the idea for *Reclamation Road* came when I was approached by a talent agency to do a reality TV show. I was intrigued, but insisted the show be about reality. I have since signed a shopping agreement with Mark Wolper and Wolper Studios at Warner Bros. They have approached a lot of television channels, but as of yet no deal has been offered. The ironic part of shopping a real show to the reality show market is that it does not contain the false suspense of the "reality show" set. It doesn't have the dumb-and-dumber appeal or the "will we make enough money here to afford another episode" sensibility. The Oprah Winfrey Network liked the show, but was disappointed that I was male and Caucasian.

Talkin' story with George Snyder, an ancient mortar and pestle in between us, we wove the fabric of our Native American indigenous roots into the storyline of *Reclamation Road*! While I was going to be interviewing the builders and shakers of the structure we were deconstructing, George was going to dig around and find the stories of those who used the mortar and pestle before us! Sadly, that most wonderful raconteur passed away after a battle with the mighty Cancer. I have dedicated *Reclamation Road* to George Snyder's memory.

"There is enough reality in the great disappearing act of the twenty-first century: the demise of the middle class and small towns. We don't need to invent a nail-biting plot," I railed. "Come on for a drive across small-town America; I'll show you reality. Let's go check out Detroit!"

So here is one Michael "Bug" Deakin, delightedly working alongside thousands for positive, sustainable change. One way I see me accomplishing change while growing my company with and for my valuable team is implementing *Reclamation Road*.

The concept is this: We want to reverse the economic malaise of America's small towns.

Reclamation Road will choose a few of the little towns across the country that are dying because they've lost their factory and/or core businesses. We want to show them how to repurpose and reuse their empty warehouses, falling-down barns, and vacant houses. We'll teach them how to start their own Heritage Salvage, along with the templates for deconstruction, remodeling, and furniture building.

Each town probably has a couple of barely surviving woodworkers. They will collaborate with tools and plans on building furniture from reclaimed wood. There will be deconstruction jobs, metal detecting, nail pulling, cleaning and inventory; jobs in website and office management, photography, interviews, research, heritage collection, and sales.

We will engage the town's core members to establish centers for social capital, organic local food, and repurposing downtown to attract new residents.

Lessons in local shopping, banking, eating, and drinking (maybe the easiest one) will be concomitant with implementation of Heritage Salvage in each chosen location. Did you know the town bar is usually the last thing to go in a dying town? That very bar may also be the last bastion of social capital in that town. It is so much more than spreading the word of Heritage Salvage across the country (though that's not a bad thing!).

As the concept of *Reclamation Road* morphed from *Barn Again* (I really liked that name, but it was taken), I sensed there was somewhere to grow here that made sustainable, practical sense. I saw a method to grow the art of Heritage Salvage while realizing my passion. That passion is a desire to see the element of ourselves reclaim our ability to foment change in the face of corporate odds.

I think our best chance to do this, other than having our own Arab Spring, is to restart our small towns, reshaping them to depend on their own population to be their economy, reinvigorating them with materials they already have. While they're doing it, they're also rejuvenating our sense of purpose, our attachment to our mother, this big round ball that oozes life for all of us.

Barn again

Occidental builder recycles old growth redwood from aging barns and coops

Photos by JOHN O'HARA / The Chronicle

Redwood beams that were used in a mine are stacked in the yard at Heritage Salvage.

By George Snyder
SPECIAL TO THE CHRONICLE

Wood-loving bugs like to spend their time in old barns and chicken shacks eating away at the aging boards, destroying them from the inside out. Michael "Bug" Deakin, on the other hand, spends his time in old barns and chicken shacks doing just the opposite.

"I'd rather save these old guys," said the 55-year-old Occidental builder, designer and owner of Heritage Salvage, a recycling enterprise he founded six months ago. "But if I can't do that, I try to recycle them."

To Deakin the words "heritage" and "salvage" go hand in hand, along with the dozens of aging barns and chicken coops still dotting southern Sonoma County. The barns are remnants of the 1930s, '40s and '50s when the combined efforts of tens of thousands of chickens made Petaluma and its environs the "Egg Capital of the World." Although many are long gone, dozens remain, leaning against the oak-studded hillsides like arthritic old men.

Recently, Deakin pulled at a colorful, lichen-encrusted board on an old 20-by-60-foot chicken shack

Owner Michael Deakin stands in the doorway of Heritage Salvage.

he was inspecting near Cotati.

"A lot of people just tear these things down and just haul the wood away to the dump," he said. "I'm here to save what we can of the old wood, one way or the other."

The property's new owners planned to turn the barn into a greenhouse, but discovered the cost would be too high. Deakin was there to salvage the wood.

"Look at this," he continued. "This is worthy wood, old-growth redwood. You just don't find this stuff anymore. Why cut down a redwood tree when you can get this great wood with just a little effort and ingenuity?"

Deakin, a native of Nelson, British Columbia, has been building homes and other structures around Sonoma County for 17 years. One of his more notable projects was a Tuscan-style garage in Occidental for a small fleet of automobiles belonging to a member of the Theriot family, the former owners of The Chronicle.

He also built sets in Hollywood for stars, including Harrison Ford, before moving north to Sonoma County.

"That's before he got famous," Deakin added by way of modesty.

Deakin's nickname, "The Bug Man" or just "Bug,"

▶ **WOODSMAN:** *Page F5*

EMPTY DENIM

DEC. 18TH
WORLD PREMIERE
STARRING RIANNA BOWEN
MUSIC BY THE
HIGHWAY
POETS

9:45 TIL MIDNIGHT
RISIBISI
154 PETALUMA BLVD N
PETALUMA
1ST SHOWING AT 10:10

RECLAMATION ROAD

ABOVE: *Sebastian and Mary Zovich on camera and concept;* **BELOW:** *Star Rianna Bowen;* **OPPOSITE:** *Rianna, Oona, Sebastian;* **OPPOSITE FAR RIGHT:** *Oona and Athena on makeup with Rianna.*

"We travel together, passengers on a little spaceship, dependent upon its vulnerable reserves of air and soil, all committed for our safety to its security and peace; preserved from annihilation only by the care, the work, and, I will say, the love we give our fragile craft. We cannot maintain it half fortunate, half miserable, half confident, half despairing, half slave to the ancient enemies of man, half free in a liberation of resources undreamed of until this day. No craft, no crew can travel safely with such vast contradictions. On their resolution depends the survival of us all."
—Adlai Stevenson, 1964

Theme Song

Empty Denim
(*Reclamation Road theme – see video*)

I found a pair of jeans
Nobody in 'em
They resonated
Of empty denim

I rubbed my knees
Where the threads were bared
And searched the pockets
For downtown fare

I found a seam where the two sides met
And fiddled around with a coin in a bet
I rolled the cuffs and found a nickel
My cashflow was down to a trickle

Half-chorus:
*Hang on, make sure there's a cold one left
Reclamation Road will show you the rest*

Born and raised in my little town
just not enough to go around
everything I know I learned from you
now you're closing your doors
and I don't know what to do

But I got lucky in my old town
'cause Reclamation Road rolled around
They took me in and showed me a way
All us townsfolk could afford to stay

Chorus:
*Hang on, make sure there's a cold one left
Reclamation Road will show you the rest
Hang on, it's surely 'bout to turn around
Reclamation Road is comin' to your town*

Bridge:
*Now get out your duds
and your empty jeans . . .
call your naybors and plant your beans
reuse, revive, reclaim, rejoice*

Chorus:
*Hang on, make sure there's a cold one left
Reclamation Road will show you the rest*

When you grow up in your small town
And you feel it all coming down
The factory left . . . the stores are gone
And the tavern is now the only one

(Chorus with vamp twice)

RECLAMATION ROAD

WE'VE ALWAYS BEEN IN THE BALLPARK AND NOW WE'RE RIGHT BEHIND HOME PLATE

HERITAGE |HS2| SALVAGE

HERITAGESALVAGE.COM

RECLAIMED BUILDING MATERIALS & CUSTOM FURNITURE

CATCH US AT- 144 C KING ST - 94107

Whale Brain

In one demonstration of our arrogance in using the entire planet and her species as fodder for our endless appetite, be it fuel or food, we are still killing whales at an alarming rate. Sadly, these highly intelligent, sentient beings are still being treated as food!

I cannot forget walking into Dr. Paul Spong's office at the University of British Columbia, where he brought down a jar with a human brain and placed it beside a huge cylinder holding the brain of a killer whale (*Orcinus orca*). It has affected me all my life.

If this inspires one person to go out and campaign on behalf of our fellow beings, then this book has done its job. Too often we campaign, throw our voices out there in unison to promote another cause, only to be engulfed by the warp speed of daily life and leave the issue floundering on the carpet of good intentions.

Jack Kerouac at Gary Snyder's going away party, May 1956 - six weeks before...

THIS PAGE: *Reclamation Road on the road!* OPPOSITE FAR LEFT: *Heritage Salvage opens second site, behind AT&T Park;* OPPOSITE LEFT: *Paul Spong and Orca.*

We cannot vote against the likes of Goldman Sachs, Bank of America, or Exxon Mobil—no matter whom we vote for. But we can mitigate their direct bearing on our well-being by taking control of as many as possible of the things we need to live.

Our food sources are greatly enhanced by our participation in their cultivation. Organic gardening defies the great Monsanto plan just by doing it.

An activist takes actions. Actions that embrace our ability to change our circumstances speak louder than words. Actions that can change our swaggering opinion that we are better than our fellow beings on this planet, and therefore entitled to as many of the resources as we see fit. This sense of entitlement, beyond paying no heed to the life that shares this planet with us, is seriously unsustainable. We are on the path to severely limiting our stay on this lovely orb.

There are so many who have no idea what it is like to live a rural life. Let's take back rural America. Let's plant the seeds of our future. While the Koch Brothers spend over $60 million smackers bankrolling the climate-change-denial groups because they are among the ten largest polluters, we watch the year 2014 bring unprecedented climate change to our planet.

Our path to Occupy is somewhat occluded by the vanishing textile of what was the middle class. The Corporate Government of America, the result of capitalism morphed into institutional corporatism, will not brook disruptions such as Occupy. Shall we stand by while the fields of the middle class are left fallow? Do we have the gumption for our own Arab Spring, or does the fact that one can buy a burger at McDonald's for $1 and pay for it from a plastic bank account keep the uprising at bay?

The uprising/protest/can't-take-it-anymore department can no longer be satisfied with indignant posture; it must take action. And the best activist action is to accentuate the positive. So, let's take back the countryside—the corporations have the guvmint already.

REPURPOSING YESTERDAY'S BEAUTIES

HERITAGE SALVAGE

RECLAIMED
HS
BUILDING MATERIALS

HERITAGESALVAGE.COM

HERITAGESALVAGE.COM

HERITAGESALVAGE.COM

INTO BEAUTIFUL TOMORROWS

No company with such a textured presence is complete without her graphic artists . . . from early days of Mary Zovich to many moons with Andrea Raschke and now firmly ensconced with the Young Nomad—Tyler Young indeed! Bless you all!

PETALUMA BLVD SO.

SAN FRANC 215 15TH STREET

NOW SERVING DESSERT

Chocolate Acacia and Mango
with Walnut Exotic slabs from Planet Earth
Custom tables – Counters – Islands – Hand Made
We also carry flooring & hand hewn beams.

HER MOTHER WAS RAISED IN A BARN & HER FATHER WAS BIG IN THE WINE BUSINESS.

HERITAGE SALVAGE
NAME
Bay Laurel
DATE OF BIRTH:
10-5-1920

HERITAGE:
Her roots are at
Madrona Manor
- Healdsburg
She's a table
traveling to
Farmhouse Local
- Larkspur
- opening Novem[

HERITAGE SALVAGE
NAME OF CHAIR:
Addi
DATE OF BIRTH:
5-10-12

HERITAGE:
**80% Foppiano
Wine Tank Wood**

20% BARN PLANKS

Everything we make has a story to tell.
We know you'll love the heritage as much as the product. No two pieces
are the same except for the fact that they'll be with you for a lifetime.
Visit www.heritagesalvage.com and start practicing sustainable enthusiasm!

AFTERWORD

Michael "Bug" Deakin is a guy who loves wood, especially big redwood beams or divinely weathered barn planks beautified from long seasons of kissing wind, the rain, and countless days of bleaching summer sun.

But as much as he loves old wood, Bug likes living trees, as well as the natural world, even more.

That in fact is one of the basic motivations of his successful "repurposing" business—Heritage Salvage—founded in the chicken coop complex it outgrew a few years ago. Recycle old, dead wood to help protect the living.

From there, Heritage Salvage has evolved into an ever-changing place for turning old things like barn wood and rusting factory gear into new things like tables, restaurant furniture, and other highly creative constructions.

Of course, few things come out of the past without a story, which is where the "heritage" part kicks in to complement the "salvage" part of his efforts, with the history of each recycled piece woven into its new life.

This sustainable enthusiasm for recycling the valuables of the past includes community outreach into the future, reaching from his base in Petaluma to the far reaches of the Midwest.

There, in his Reclamation Road project, dying farming towns would do well to heed Bug's advice in order to help turn what has become old and forgotten into what can be renewed and sustainable.

That's Bug's story—and I'm sure he's sticking to it.

George Snyder

George Snyder, a longtime Chronicle *North Bay reporter and dedicated conservationist, died January 10, 2013, after a long battle with pancreatic cancer. He was sixty-eight. Friends and family remembered the lanky figure—who regularly wore cowboy hats and boots and a trademark grin—for both his committed journalism and his love of nature.*

ABOVE: *George Snyder;* **OPPOSITE, FAR RIGHT TOP:** *Reclamation Road Radio, on The Drive with Jaxon, KSRO 1350, Tuesdays 5:30 – 6 pm.*

ACKNOWLEDGMENTS

I would like to thank Gary Starr for first suggesting I do a book that would help generate interest in Heritage Salvage, Mary Nova Zovich for jumping on board and helping me with the initial design and layout, Andrea Raschke for all the graphics she has done for HS over the years, Lorna Johnson for her enthusiasm and publishing knowledge, Vikki MacDonald for sending me a great collection of newspaper articles, and then !!!!!! Douglas Gayeton for telling Cameron and Company that I was doing a book and introducing me to same! Chris Gruener for believing it would be worth publishing, Iain Morris for taking the scrapbook of my life and making it beautiful, and Mark "W. Rabbit" Burstein for dealing with my quirky run-on stream-of-unconsciousness writing style and making it make sense!

At this point I would LOVE to acknowledge every friend I have known, and every being that has touched me for even a moment, every chance meeting, every incident that has changed me . . . it would have to be a never-ending book to include you all. The landlords, the tenants, the customers, the antagonists, the believers and the soothsayers, the adventurers and the masters of the word, the pets and the wild ones, you are all a part of this book because you are all a part of me. Every time you turn a corner life can change . . . the essence of change is the capacity to reinvent . . . regrets are excess baggage . . . get out there and try everything!

Life is a set of circumstances . . . love is a many splendored thing.

Certificate for Most Creative

Professional Division
Awarded at the Habitat for Humanity of Sonoma County
"Habitat is Doggone Green" Event on April 21, 2007

Name: Heritage Salvage

①Rough sawn skip planed Redwood top
②Slightly tapered legs notched at the
③ ...

COLOPHON

CAMERON + COMPANY
Publisher: *Chris Gruener*
Creative Director & Design:
Iain R. Morris
Editor: *Mark Burstein*
Copyeditor: *Michelle Dotter*

The publisher would like to thank Bug for allowing us the opportunity to salvage his own heritage in the form of a book; Mark Burstein for his incredible organization and editorial work; Iain Morris for somehow managing to put all of these images and stories into a beautiful book; and Michelle Dotter for her pinpoint copy editing.

All text ©2014 Michael Deakin. All images ©2014 except where noted; all images © by Michael Deakin except for pp. 20–21: Richard Sifton; 32 (Catriona, DNA): from *Partnering with Nature* ©2010 Catriona MacGregor; 33 (illustrations): John O'Neill; 35: painting by John Hudson ©1998; 36 (flyer), 74 (shiplap profile, flooring ad), 79 (collage), 163 (collage 2nd from right, top): Andrea Rashcke; 44, 111, 118: sketches by Chris Cheek; 47: Jennifer Sauer; 50–51, 54–61, 70–71, 78–80, 81 (except Waldo sign), 82–86, 88–89, 96–97, 102–103, 106–107, 150–151: Tyler Chartier Architectural Photography; 62, 63, 64 (except top two left), 65: Frankie Frankeny/©frankenyimages.com; 72, 74: Scott Hess Photography; 73, 168 (top right): Paige Green Photography; 75, 142 (the Clementines), 162 (photo in ad by Tyler Young), 168 (bottom left): Michael Woolsey; 91–93: Eric Rorer Photography (except the one of Liz and me); 112 (Moshin images): Amber Moshin; 113: Flora Grubb Gardens; 137 (collage), 144 (ad), 153 (bottom right), 164–165 (3 ads across top): Mary Zovich; 138 (Rivertown poster), 160 (empty denim poster), 164–165 (large ads), 168 (HS2 ad): Tyler Young/Young Nomad; 141 (top left, top middle, 2nd from top on right, and sailor Chris "No Hell" Aluia), 142 (top right, bottom right, Kelin and Green Mary): Joan Bunn; 143 (poster): Sebastian Nau; 162 (Paul Spong): Peter Thomas; 163 (RR in Europe): Rianna Bowen.

CUSTOM DESIGN
CREATIVE REPURPOSING
RECLAIMED BUILDING MATERIALS

HERITAGE SALVAGE

FURNITURE AND STORIES
YOU WILL LOVE TO LIVE WITH

PETALUMA
1473 PETALUMA BLVD S
HERITAGESALVAGE.COM
707 762-6277

SAN FRANCISCO
NOW 2,000 SQ FT
215 15TH ST AT KANSAS
HERITAGESALVAGE.COM/SANFRANCISCO
415 255-8598

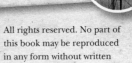

CAMERON + COMPANY

6 Petaluma Blvd. North, Suite B-6
Petaluma, CA 94952

(707) 769-1617
www.cameronbooks.com

Library of Congress Control Number: 2014934497

ISBN: 978-1-937359-50-8

Printed and bound in China

10 9 8 7 6 5 4 3 2 1

greener E

RECLAMATION ROAD

WOOD TALKS

3 x 3